Overcoming Grief:

Surviving the Death of a Spouse –
A Christian Perspective

Janice A. Campbell

Copyright

Copyright © 2025 by Janice A. Campbell

The content contained within this book may not be reproduced, duplicated or transmitted without direct written permission from the author or the publisher.

Under no circumstances will any blame or legal responsibility be held against the publisher or author for any damages, reparation, or monetary loss due to the information contained within this book, either directly or indirectly.

Legal Notice:

This book is copyright-protected. It is only for personal use. You cannot amend, distribute, sell, use, quote, or paraphrase any part, or the content within this book, without the consent of the author or publisher.

Scripture quotations taken from The Holy Bible, New International Version® NIV®Copyright © 1973, 1978, 1984, 2011 by Biblica, Inc.Used with permission. All rights reserved worldwide.

<u>Disclaimer Notice:</u>

Please note the information contained within this document is for educational and entertainment purposes only. All effort has been executed to present accurate, up-to-date, reliable, complete information. No warranties of any kind are declared or implied. Readers acknowledge that the author is not engaged in the rendering of legal, financial, medical or professional advice. The content within this book has been derived from various sources. Please consult a licensed professional before attempting any techniques outlined in this book.

By reading this document, the reader agrees that under no circumstances is the author responsible for any losses, direct or indirect, that are incurred as a result of the use of the information contained within this document, including, but not limited to, errors, omissions, or inaccuracies.

Printed in the United States of America.

First Edition: January 2025

Contact the author: wealthhealthforever@hotmail.com

Contents

FORWARD ... 1

Introduction: Facing the Unimaginable ... 2
   Understanding Grief:
   The Void of Losing a Spouse:
   Why This Book?
   Setting Expectations: A Journey Without a Map
   Why Your Grief Matters
   You Are Not Alone

Part I: The Immediate Aftermath ... 9

Chapter 1: The Shock of Loss ... 10
   Initial Reactions:
   First Steps:
   The Fog of Early Grief

   Support in the Early Days:
   Permission to Grieve
   A Glimmer of Light

Chapter 2: Surviving the First Few Weeks   19
   Emotional Overload
   Caring for Yourself
   Moments of Joy and Guilt for Feeling Them
   Navigating the Emotional Rollercoaster
   Finding Support:
   Embracing the Complexity of Grief

Part 2: Understanding Grief   27

Chapter 3: The Many Faces of Grief   28
   Stages of Grief:
   Limitations and Adaptations
   Physical Manifestations of Grief
   Secondary Losses:
   Individual Differences:
   Spiritual and Existential Questions
   The Fluidity of Grief

Chapter 4: How Love Shapes Loss   42
   A Unique Grief:
   The Loneliness of Absence

Part 3: Navigating Change and Growth   49

Chapter 5: Rebuilding a Life After Loss   50
  Navigating the Practical Realities
  Coping with Emotional Adjustments
  Rediscovering Your Identity
  Finding a New Normal
  Honoring the Journey

Chapter 6: Cultivating Resilience and   57
Hope
  What is Resilience?
  The Role of Hope in Healing
  Practical Strategies for Cultivating Resilience
  Stories of Resilience
  Embracing the Possibility of Joy
  Looking Ahead

Chapter 7: Keeping Memories Alive   65
  Why We Remember
  Personal Ways to Honor Their Memory
  Balancing Remembrance and Moving Forward
  When Remembrance Becomes Overwhelming
  Living Their Legacy
  Embracing a Future Rooted in Love

Chapter 8: Finding Meaning After Loss   73
   Why Meaning Matters
   The Many Paths to Meaning
   Transforming Grief Into Purpose
   Embracing Change
   The Role of Gratitude
   Stories of Transformation
   Finding Meaning Is a Process

Chapter 9: Approaching Uncertainty with   82
Grace
   Understanding the Nature of Uncertainty
   Building Resilience in the Face of Uncertainty
   Strategies for Embracing the Unknown
   Finding Hope Amid Uncertainty
   Lessons from Uncertainty
   Looking Forward with Grace

Chapter 10: Rediscovering Joy and Purpose   92
   Understanding Joy After Loss
   Defining a New Sense of Purpose
   Reconnecting with Others
   Balancing Reflection and Forward Movement

    Gratitude as a Bridge to Healing
    Faith and Gratitude

Chapter 14: Finding Purpose Anew   124
    Understanding the Void
    Purpose in the Midst of Grief
    Embracing Change
    The Role of Faith in Rediscovering Purpose
    Purpose Through Service
    Finding Joy Again
    The Legacy of Love
    A Journey Toward Renewal

Chapter 15: What Happens at Death? A   133
Biblical Perspective
    The Origin of Death
    The Condition of the Dead
    Trust in God, Not in Humanity
    The Hope Beyond Death
    A Source of Comfort
    Conclusion

Chapter 16: Reflection and Growth   139
    The Power of Reflection
    Lessons Learned Along the Way
    Carrying Growth into the Future
    A Journey That Continues

    Signs of Renewal
    Stories of Renewal
    Looking Forward with Hope

Chapter 11: Rediscovering Your Identity   101
    The Void Left Behind
    Allowing Yourself to Mourn the Changes
    The Role of Faith in Rediscovery
    Steps Toward Rediscovery
    A New Chapter Begins

Chapter 12: Building Self-Confidence After a Loss   108
    The Impact of Loss on Self-Confidence
    Biblical Encouragement for Strength and Courage
    Steps to Rebuild Self-Confidence
    Addressing Fear and Anxiety
    Celebrating Progress
    Conclusion: Confidence Rooted in Faith

Chapter 13: The Role of Gratitude in Healing   116
    The Paradox of Gratitude in Grief
    How Gratitude Heals
    Finding Gratitude in Shared Love
    Practical Ways to Cultivate Gratitude

Closing Reflections

Chapter 17: The Resurrection Hope 145
    The Biblical Foundation of the Resurrection Hope
    How the Resurrection Hope Comforts Grieving Hearts
    Living in the Light of the Resurrection Hope
    Stories of Resurrection Hope
    A Closing Word of Hope

Conclusion: A Journey, Not a Destination 152
    Honoring the Past, Embracing the Future
    The Role of Faith and Hope
    A New Perspective on Life
    The Journey Continues
    A Final Word of Hope

About the Author 157

FORWARD

I am writing about my experiences surrounding the death of my loved ones. I have endured the death of both my parents and my older sister, but by far the worst experience was the death of my husband James. We married later in life and had 17 years together. Because I have found that the death of my husband was by far the most profound grief I have experienced, I have chosen to write about that grief experience. In addition to being a survivor of grief, I am a Christian minister and will draw on and share my knowledge of the Bible, as it has considerably eased the pain of my grief.

Introduction: Facing the Unimaginable

Understanding Grief:

Grief is a universal experience, yet it feels deeply personal when it happens to you. The loss of a spouse—the person who shared your dreams, your struggles, and your everyday moments—is one of the most profound losses a human being can endure. It's a loss that shakes the foundation of your world, leaving you to navigate a life that suddenly feels foreign and incomplete. If you are reading this book, you are likely grappling with that unimaginable pain. Please know that you are not alone.

This book was born out of the desire to provide solace, understanding, and guidance to those walking the difficult path of grieving a spouse. While grief is a profoundly individual journey, there are common threads in the experience that can help you feel connected to others who have faced similar losses. There is no "right" way to grieve, but there are tools and insights that can offer comfort and light, even in the darkest of times.

The Void of Losing a Spouse:

The loss of a spouse is unlike any other. This person was likely your confidant, teammate, and closest companion. Together, you shared a life that was uniquely yours—a collection of shared routines, inside jokes, and intimate moments that no one else fully understands. When they are gone, it's not just their absence you grieve, but also the loss of the life you built together and the future you imagined. The ripple effects of such a loss touch every aspect of your existence. The person who shared every day of your life is now gone; with them is gone the vision of the rest of your life. Your daily routine is shattered. Perhaps, too, your sense of security and normalcy are gone as well. Rest assured that over time, these will return. Over time, you will develop a new understanding of security built on self-reliance and resiliency. And your sense of normalcy will return, although your daily life will be built on a new normal without your spouse.

In the early days of grief, it's common to feel as though the world has stopped, even as it continues to move forward for everyone else. Tasks that once felt simple—getting out of bed, eating a meal, answering a phone call—may now feel insurmountable. Emotions like sadness, anger, guilt, and confusion may crash over you in waves, often without warning. This book aims to provide a steady hand to hold as you face these overwhelming moments, offering practical advice and emotional support.

Why This Book?

The journey through grief is deeply personal, and no single book can provide all the answers. However, this book aims to be a compassionate companion, offering guidance and reassurance as you navigate this uncharted territory. You will find:

- **Practical Advice:** From handling the immediate responsibilities after your spouse's passing to adjusting to life on your own, this book provides actionable steps to help you manage the practicalities of loss.

- **Emotional Insights:** Grief is messy and nonlinear. This book explores the emotional complexities of grieving a spouse, helping you understand that your feelings—whatever they may be—are valid.

- **Tools for Healing:** From journaling prompts to mindfulness exercises, this book offers tools to help you process your grief and rebuild your life.

Setting Expectations: A Journey Without a Map

One of the most challenging aspects of grief is its unpredictability. It does not follow a neat timeline or a prescribed set of stages. Some days, you may feel a glimmer of hope or peace, only to be blindsided by sorrow the next. This ebb and flow is a natural part of the process, though it can feel disorienting.

This book does not promise quick fixes or easy answers. Instead, it offers an invitation to take things one step at a time. Grief is not something to be "gotten over" but to be carried and integrated into your life. Over time, the weight of that grief will lessen, and you will find moments of joy and connection again.

Why Your Grief Matters

In a world that often pressures people to "move on" or "stay strong," it's important to recognize that your grief is a testament to your love. The depth of your pain reflects the depth of your connection to your spouse. It's okay to mourn, to cry, and to feel lost. This book reminds you that those feelings are not signs of weakness but humanity.

Grieving a spouse also brings with it unique challenges. Friends and family may struggle to understand the depth of your loss, especially if they have never experienced a similar bereavement. Well-meaning advice or platitudes can sometimes feel hurtful or dismissive. This book acknowledges and guides how to navigate those challenges with grace, forgiveness, and self-compassion.

You Are Not Alone

In the pages ahead, you will find a blend of practical advice and emotional support. These elements are designed to meet you wherever you are in your grief—whether you are in the early days of shock and numbness, or further along in your journey, seeking ways to rebuild your life and find meaning in everyday life without your mate.

Grief can feel isolating, but you are not alone. There is a community of people who understand the pain of losing a spouse. By opening this book, you are taking an essential step toward healing. While the journey may be long and arduous, it is also a testament to the love you shared and the resilience within you.

As you turn the page and begin this journey, remember that grief is not a destination but a process. There is no timeline, no roadmap, and no "right" way to do this. But with time, patience, and support, it is possible to find a way forward. Your life will never be the same, but it can still hold meaning, connection, and even joy. Let this book be a guiding light as you navigate the darkness, reminding you that you are not alone and that healing is possible in its own time and way.

Part I: The Immediate Aftermath

Chapter 1: The Shock of Loss

Initial Reactions:

None of us is prepared for the death of our spouse. Even if they are sick with a life-threatening illness, we are not prepared for the moment of death. That is because humans were originally created to live forever. The death of humans was not part of God's original purpose. God instructed Adam not to eat from the tree of the knowledge of good and evil under penalty of death. (Genesis 2:16, 17) Later, Adam and Eve ate from the forbidden tree and sinned against God, bringing sin and death to all of their imperfect descendants. (Genesis 3:1-6; Romans 5:12) This explains why we experience such profound grief at the death of a loved one. We were not created to experience their death. But the fact remains that until after Armageddon, we will continue to be plagued by death and have to endure the death of our dear loved ones. (Revelation 21:3-5) Hence the need for this book.

When God created Eve, he designed woman to be a mate for man and a helper to him. (Genesis 2:18) God went on to bring Eve to Adam and perform the first marriage in the Garden of Eden. (Genesis 2:22-24) Since marriage was designed to yoke two souls together as one, it is not surprising that the death of one's spouse causes a profound loss and grief in their life. Many who have lost a spouse in death express the feeling of loss as if they had lost a part of themselves, like an arm or a leg. Given that man and woman were created to be lifelong monogamous mates, it is no wonder that the loss of a mate causes profound grief.

First Steps:

In the initial moments after losing your spouse, you may find yourself in a state of shock and disbelief. Even if the loss was anticipated, the finality of death often feels surreal. The person who was your anchor, your life partner, is suddenly no longer there. The emotional and physical reactions to this realization can be overwhelming, and it's common to feel as though the world has reached a standstill.

Grief often begins with a wave of numbness or disbelief. You might wake up expecting your spouse to still be there, only to be jolted by the painful reality that they are indeed gone. This reaction is your mind's way of protecting you from the full weight of your loss. It's okay if you don't immediately feel the depth of your emotions. The death of a spouse can leave you in an initial state of emotional shock. You may also experience a period of overwhelming sadness that manifests as uncontrollable crying. Everyone processes loss differently, and there is no right or wrong way to feel.

You may also experience physical symptoms during this time, such as fatigue, difficulty sleeping, loss of appetite, or even physical pain. These reactions are your body's response to the immense stress of grief. If you feel overwhelmed, remember that what you're experiencing is a natural response to an extraordinary loss.

At this difficult time, you need to practice self-care without feeling guilty.

- **Handling Financial and Legal Matters:** In the immediate aftermath, you may need to address paperwork such as death certificates, insurance claims, or your spouse's will. These tasks can feel impersonal and emotionally taxing, but tackling them step by step can help prevent future complications. It can be very helpful to enlist the assistance of a trusted friend or family member to accompany you while you deal with these necessary matters.

If these responsibilities feel insurmountable, remember that you don't have to face them alone. Lean on your support network or consider reaching out to a grief counselor or other professionals who can guide you through the process.

The Fog of Early Grief

In the days and weeks following your loss, you might find yourself moving through life in a fog. This state of mind is common and can make even the simplest tasks feel challenging. You may find your-

In the midst of your emotional pain, there are practical matters that demand your attention. These tasks can feel daunting, especially when you're in shock. However, they are necessary steps that can provide a sense of structure during an otherwise chaotic time. It is wise to write things down as your memory may be unreliable during this time of grief. Common responsibilities include:

- **Notifying Loved Ones:** Sharing the news of your spouse's passing can be one of the most challenging tasks. Enlist a trusted friend or family member to help make calls or send messages if it feels too overwhelming. Family and friends may not realize the toll the death of your mate places on you, so don't be shy about communicating your need for support and assistance at this time.

- **Arranging a Funeral or Memorial:** Planning a service can be both a burden and a healing experience. It's a chance to honor your partner's life, but it can also bring intense emotions to the surface. In your current emotional state, you may not be up to the task of coordinating the funeral arrangements. If this is the case, don't hesitate to ask for help from friends, family, or funeral professionals.

self forgetting things, struggling to concentrate, or feeling detached from the world around you. This is your mind's way of processing an overwhelming loss, and it's a sign that you need to give yourself grace. Feelings of anger at the situation or guilt because of your inability to handle matters on your own may surface. Remember that these feelings are common symptoms of grief, and you need to have compassion for yourself.

Focus on small, manageable tasks during this time. Take each day as it comes, and don't pressure yourself to function at your usual capacity. If all you can do in a day is get out of bed or make a meal, that's enough. Allow yourself the space to grieve.

Support in the Early Days:

Grieving the loss of a spouse can feel incredibly isolating, but you don't have to go through it alone. Reaching out to others can provide comfort and practical assistance during this difficult time. Consider the following sources of support:

- **Family and Friends:** Loved ones may not always know what to say or do, but many want to help. Be honest about your needs, whether it's someone to listen, run errands, or simply sit with you in silence. Others who have not experienced a similar loss may not comprehend the depth of your grief, but if you can communicate your needs, they will likely be glad to assist.

- **Grief Counselors and Therapists:** A professional can offer tools and techniques to help you process your emotions and navigate your loss. Don't hesitate to seek their guidance if you're struggling.

- **Support Groups:** Connecting with others who have experienced a similar loss can help you feel less alone. Sharing your story and hearing others' experiences can provide comfort and perspective.

Permission to Grieve

One of the most important things to remember in these early days is that it's okay to grieve in your own way. Society often imposes expectations about how grief should look or how long it should last, but your journey is uniquely yours. Allow yourself to feel whatever emotions arise, whether it's sadness, anger, guilt, or even moments of relief.

Grief is not a linear process, and there is no timeline for healing. In these initial moments, focus on surviving each day as it comes. There will be time to explore the deeper layers of your grief and begin the work of healing, but for now, it's enough to exist with your pain.

A Glimmer of Light

Though the shock of loss can feel overwhelming, know that you will not always feel this way. The pain of grief may never entirely disappear, but it will evolve and lessen over time. Moments of joy, connection, and hope will begin to reemerge, even if they feel impossible to imagine now. For now, take each moment as it comes, and trust that healing is possible in its own time.

As you navigate this initial stage of grief, let this chapter serve as a reminder that you are not alone. The journey ahead may be long and difficult, but it is also a testament to the love you shared and the strength you carry within you. Lean on your support system, honor your emotions, and take things one day at a time. This is only the beginning of your healing journey.

Chapter 2: Surviving the First Few Weeks

Emotional Overload

Grief is not a single emotion but a complex and ever-changing tapestry of feelings. In the wake of losing your spouse, you may find yourself overwhelmed by a range of emotions, many of which can feel contradictory. One moment, you might feel deep sorrow, and the next, a sense of anger or even numbness. Understanding the breadth of these emotions and allowing yourself to experience them without judgment is a crucial step in your grieving journey.

Sadness and Longing

Perhaps the most immediate and pervasive emotion after loss is sadness. The absence of your spouse's presence—their voice, touch, and companionship—can leave an aching void. You might find yourself longing for just one more conversation or one more moment together. You may find, at the times that you can sleep, that your dreams are filled with images of your spouse. These feelings of sadness and yearning are natural responses to the depth of your love and the connection you shared.

During these times, you may find solace in small rituals or moments of reflection. Looking at photographs, writing letters to your loved one, or revisiting cherished memories can help you honor your relationship and process your sorrow. While these activities can bring a sense of comfort, it's also okay to step away if they feel too painful in the moment. Remember that photographs and other memorabilia will be there when you are ready to reflect on cherished memories. Another ritual that sometimes brings comfort is to talk about your spouse with friends and family that knew them well.

Anger and Resentment

Anger is another common but often misunderstood emotion in grief. You may feel anger at the unfairness of your loss, at the circumstances surrounding your spouse's death, or even at your spouse for leaving you. These feelings can be unsettling, especially if you're someone who doesn't typically experience anger. It's important to remember that anger is a natural and valid part of grief.

Rather than suppressing these feelings, try to explore their source. Journaling, talking with a trusted friend, or working with a therapist can help you process your anger in a healthy way. Sometimes, expressing your anger physically—through activities like exercise or even punching a pillow—can provide relief.

Guilt and Regret

Feelings of guilt and regret often accompany the loss of a spouse. You might find yourself replaying moments in your relationship, wondering if you could have done something differently. "What if" questions can become a relentless refrain: "What if I had noticed the signs earlier?" or "What if I had been more patient or loving?"

It's important to acknowledge these feelings without letting them consume you. No relationship is perfect, and it's likely that your spouse cherished you for who you were, imperfections and all. Talking through these feelings with a counselor or trusted friend can help you find perspective and self-forgiveness.

Caring for Yourself

At times, you may feel emotionally numb or detached from the world around you. This can be disorienting, especially if you're used to being in touch with your emotions. Numbness is your mind's way of shielding you from the pain that feels too overwhelming to process all at once.

During these periods, it's important to practice self-compassion. Don't force yourself to feel or act a certain way. Instead, focus on small, grounding activities like taking a walk, listening to calming music, or engaging in simple, repetitive tasks like knitting or journaling your feelings. It is crucial that you don't neglect your basic self-care, like adequate rest and nutrition. Sleeping may be difficult at this time, especially if you slept beside your spouse. If sleeping at night in your shared bed is challenging, try napping during the day in a recliner or on the sofa in the living room. Over time, as you process your grief, moments of numbness will likely give way to a fuller range of emotions.

Moments of Joy and Guilt for Feeling Them

Amidst the sadness and pain, you may experience brief moments of joy or relief. Perhaps a fond memory makes you smile, or you find yourself laughing at something your spouse would have enjoyed. These moments can bring a sense of comfort, but they might also trigger feelings of guilt. You may wonder if it's too soon to feel happy or if experiencing joy means you're forgetting your spouse.

It's important to recognize that moments of joy are not a betrayal of your spouse. They are a testament to the resilience of the human spirit and the love you shared. Allow yourself to feel these moments fully, without guilt. They are a sign that gradual healing is beginning to take place.

Navigating the Emotional Rollercoaster

Grief does not follow a straight path. Instead, it often feels like a rollercoaster of emotions, with highs and lows that can be unpredictable. In the Kubler-Ross model, the stages of grief are defined as denial, anger, bargaining, depression, and acceptance. However, these emotions don't occur in a neat progression because grief is not linear. On some days, you may feel a sense of peace or acceptance, only to be blindsided by sorrow or anger the next. This nonlinear nature of grief can be frustrating, but it's also a reminder that healing is not a rigid process.

To navigate this emotional turbulence, try to:

- **Acknowledge Your Feelings:** Whatever you feel in the moment, allow yourself to experience it without judgment.

- **Find Healthy Outlets:** Activities like journaling, art, or exercise can provide a constructive way to express your emotions.

- **Seek Support:** Talking with others who understand your pain can help you feel less alone. If you feel ready, seek the comfort a grief support group can provide.

- **Be Patient with Yourself:** Healing takes time, and it's okay to have good days and bad days.

Finding Support:

If your emotions feel too overwhelming to manage on your own, consider reaching out to a grief counselor or therapist. Professional support can provide tools and techniques to help you process your feelings and move forward in your grief journey. Remember, seeking help is not a sign of weakness but of strength, self-awareness, and self-care.

Embracing the Complexity of Grief

Grief is as unique as the love you shared with your mate. It encompasses a wide range of emotions, each one a reflection of the depth of your connection. By embracing these feelings and allowing yourself to move through them, you honor both your grief and your love. The path through these emotions may be difficult, but it is also a testament to your resilience and capacity for healing.

In the chapters ahead, we will explore practical tools and strategies to help you navigate life after loss. For now, let this chapter serve as a reminder that all your feelings—whether painful or comforting—are valid. In giving yourself permission to feel, you take the first steps toward integrating your grief into a life that still holds meaning, connection, and hope.

Part 2: Understanding Grief

Chapter 3: The Many Faces of Grief

Grief is a deeply personal and multifaceted experience. It encompasses a wide range of emotions, thoughts, and physical sensations, each reflecting the profound impact of your loss. In this chapter, we explore the various forms grief can take, providing insight into the complexity of the grieving process.

Stages of Grief:

The Kübler-Ross model, introduced by psychiatrist Elisabeth Kübler-Ross in her 1969 book *On Death and Dying*, offers a framework for understanding the emotional process of grief. Initially developed to describe the stages experienced by terminally ill patients, it has since been widely applied to anyone dealing with loss, including the death of a loved one, divorce, job loss, or other life-altering events. The model outlines five stages of grief: denial, anger, bargaining, depression, and acceptance. While these stages provide insight into the grieving process, it's important to note that grief is not a linear experience—individuals may revisit stages, skip some, or experience them in varying orders and to varying degrees.

1. Denial

The first stage, denial, is a defense mechanism that helps individuals process the initial shock of loss. It often manifests as disbelief or numbness, as the mind struggles to comprehend the magnitude of the loss. For example, someone may think, *"This isn't happening"* or *"There must be some mistake."* Denial serves a protective purpose by allowing the person to absorb the reality of the loss gradually, preventing them from becoming overwhelmed all at once.

2. Anger

As the initial shock wears off, it is common to feel anger. This stage may involve frustration, resentment, or feelings of injustice. Individuals may direct their anger at themselves, others, or the situation, and sometimes even at the deceased or a higher power. You may feel anger towards your spouse for leaving you alone. Of course, mentally you may know that they had no choice in their death, emotionally however, you may feel a profound sense of abandonment. Common thoughts during this stage include, *"Why did this happen to me?"* or *"This isn't fair."* Anger can serve as a way to release pent-up emotions and regain a sense of control, even if temporarily.

3. Bargaining

The bargaining stage is marked by a desire to regain a sense of control or prevent further loss. Individuals often reflect on "what if" scenarios or make promises in the hope of changing the outcome. For example, a grieving person might think, *"If only I had done something differently"* or *"I will do anything to have them back."* While bargaining is often a futile attempt to change the past or influence uncontrollable outcomes, it is a natural part of the process of coming to terms with reality.

4. Depression

Depression is a natural response to profound loss and often represents the deepest stage of grieving. During this phase, individuals may experience sadness, hopelessness, withdrawal, and a lack of energy or interest in daily life. It is common to feel overwhelmed by the weight of the loss, as the permanence of the situation begins to sink in. During this stage, you may feel unable to get out of bed and you may sleep more than usual. While painful, this stage is a crucial part of grieving, allowing individuals to process their emotions and begin the healing process.

Feelings of guilt may arise here as individuals process the implications of their loss and revisit memories. Individuals might dwell on regrets, such as perceived shortcomings in their relationship with their mate They may feel responsible for things that were beyond their control, blaming themselves for the loss. Unlike bargaining, where guilt is intertwined with hypothetical scenarios, the guilt in depression is often tied to feelings of inadequacy or unresolved issues. Feelings of guilt during grief are normal but can become problematic if they turn into persistent, overwhelming self-blame. It's essential for grieving individuals to acknowledge their emotions without judging themselves harshly. Scriptural reflection can help alleviate feelings of guilt and foster acceptance. For example:

"As far as the east is from the west, so far has he removed our transgressions from us." (Psalm 103:12, NIV)

This verse reminds us of God's forgiveness, encouraging us to let go of burdens that are not ours to bear.

5. Acceptance

The final stage, acceptance, is not about being "okay" with the loss but rather about acknowledging the reality of the situation and finding a way to move forward. Acceptance involves integrating the loss into one's life and beginning to rebuild. This stage may include finding meaning in the experience, adjusting to a new normal, and embracing life despite the absence of the loved one. During the initial shock of your loss, it may feel like you will never reach a stage of acceptance, know that, in time, you will get there. Rebuilding your life without your spouse is a difficult process but one that you will inevitably face and conquer during your healing process.

Limitations and Adaptations

While the Kübler-Ross model provides valuable insight, it is not a one-size-fits-all approach. Grief is highly personal, and individuals may not experience all the stages or may navigate them in a different order. Modern interpretations of the model emphasize its flexibility, encouraging individuals to honor their unique grief journey rather than adhere strictly to its framework.

In recognizing the stages of grief, individuals gain a sense of validation and understanding for their emotions. It helps normalize the complex and often unpredictable process of grieving, offering a roadmap while acknowledging the individuality of the journey. Although each person's grief journey is unique, there are certain commonalities that individuals experience. As you recognize your own experiences of the stages of grief it helps you to know that what you are going through is a normal reaction to an extraordinary loss.

The emotional intensity of grief can be overwhelming. It may manifest as sadness, anger, guilt, or even relief, depending on the circumstances of your loss. These emotions often come in waves, sometimes triggered by a memory, a familiar scent, or a specific date. As your progress through your grief journey, know that certain dates like your wedding anniversary, your spouse's birthday and the anniversary of your spouse's death may be especially difficult days. You may experience feelings of sadness, loss and depression around these particular dates even years after the loss of your spouse. But as these special dates pass by, you should return to your new normal emotionally. Know that these brief periods of renewed grief should lessen over time.

- **Sadness and Longing:** Sadness is a natural response to the absence of your spouse. You may find yourself yearning for their presence, longing for one more conversation or shared moment.

- **Anger and Resentment:** You might feel anger at the unfairness of your loss, at circumstances surrounding their death, or even at your spouse for leaving you. This anger is not something to fear but to explore as part of your healing.

- **Guilt and Regret:** Many grieving individuals replay moments of their relationship, questioning decisions or actions. "What if" and "if only" thoughts can weigh heavily, but acknowledging and addressing these feelings can pave the way for forgiveness and understanding.

Physical Manifestations of Grief

Grief is not only emotional but also physical. You might experience symptoms such as fatigue, changes in appetite, difficulty remembering things, or difficulty sleeping. These physical responses are the body's way of processing the emotional toll of your loss.

- **Fatigue:** Grief can be exhausting, sapping your energy and making even simple tasks feel overwhelming. Rather than being disappointed in yourself for feeling fatigued, it is time for self-care and compassion. Seek help from your friends and family to give you the support you need to deal with necessary tasks.

- **Appetite Changes:** You might notice a loss

of appetite or, conversely, an urge to seek comfort in food. Know that this is a normal reaction to the grief you are enduring.

- **Memory Lapses:** You may experience difficulty remembering things that happened shortly after the loss of your spouse. For this reason, it is wise to write down important details that you might otherwise have difficulty remembering.

- **Sleep Disturbances:** Insomnia or restless sleep is common, as the mind struggles to process the enormity of your loss. Getting sufficient sleep is a necessary part of self-care, so if sleeping at night is difficult, try napping during the day.

Recognizing these physical manifestations as a normal part of grief can help you approach them with self-compassion. Practicing self-care, such as maintaining a balanced diet, engaging in gentle exercise, and prioritizing rest, can support your physical and emotional well-being.

Secondary Losses:

CHAPTER 3: THE MANY FACES OF GRIEF 37

Grief can also affect your thoughts and behaviors, sometimes in ways that feel disorienting. These changes are a reflection of your brain's efforts to adapt to a new reality.

- **Confusion and Forgetfulness:** It's common to feel scattered or have difficulty concentrating. Grief can create a mental fog that makes it hard to focus on tasks. Periods of confusion and forgetfulness can last for quite a while. It is wise to write down important details and to enlist the assistance of a trusted friend or family member to accompany you on important appointments or when dealing with important paperwork. Because of difficulties focusing it is best to put off making important decisions until your mental faculties return to normal. This is especially true regarding important life decisions like moving your residence, selling the family home, making major purchases, etc. These major life decisions are better left until you have made major strides in healing from your grief.

- **Reliving Memories:** You may find yourself revisiting moments with your spouse, both joyful and painful, as your mind works to process your loss. This is a normal pastime during the grieving process. Initially reliving memories may cause a wave of sadness and crying as you come to grips with the reality that your mate is gone. But as time goes on, reliving pleasant memories will bring back the happy feelings associated with memories shared with your spouse rather than sadness.

- **Avoidance Behaviors:** You might avoid places, activities, or conversations that remind you of your spouse, as a way of shielding yourself from pain. This avoidance behavior is especially common during the initial stages of grief when you are experiencing deep sadness or depression.

Individual Differences:

Grief often extends beyond the individual, affecting your interactions with others. Friends and family may struggle to know how to support you, and you might feel isolated in your pain. Although it may be difficult at first, try to communicate your needs for support and assistance to friends and family. Friends and family truly want to ease your grief but often need guidance in knowing how to help.

- **Changing Relationships:** Some relationships may grow stronger as loved ones rally around you and give support, while others may feel strained due to misunderstandings or discomfort with grief. As difficult as it may be while you are experiencing the depths of sorrow, try to have compassion for others in your family who are grieving the loss of your spouse. Although the depth of their loss may not be the same as yours, they are still going through the grieving process. Your in-laws are likely coping with the death of their son or daughter or the loss of their sibling. Your children are coping with the loss of their parent, and close family friends are coping with the loss of a dear friend. Emotions are running high for everyone in your close family circle, so try to be forgiving of others and compassionate.

- **Support Networks:** Joining a grief support group or seeking connection with others who have experienced similar losses can provide comfort and validation. It can sometimes be easier to express your emotions with strangers than with friends and family that are going through the grieving process.

Spiritual and Existential Questions

The loss of a spouse can prompt profound spiritual or existential questions. You might wrestle with questions about the meaning of life, the nature of love, or what happens after death.

- **Seeking Meaning:** Finding a sense of purpose or meaning in your loss can be a common theme during the healing process. This might involve honoring your spouse's legacy or redefining your own life goals.

- **Spiritual Practices:** Engaging in prayer, meditation, Bible reading or other spiritual practices can provide solace and a sense of connection to something greater than yourself. The Bible provides answers to many of the existential questions that people grapple with on losing a loved one in death.

The Fluidity of Grief

Grief is not a linear process but a dynamic and evolving experience. Some days, you may feel a sense of peace and acceptance, while others may bring waves of pain and sorrow. This unpredictability is a natural part of the journey. It is important to give yourself permission to experience your feelings however they come.

Building a Life Amidst Grief

Grieving does not mean abandoning joy or hope. It is about learning to carry your loss alongside the life you continue to build. By acknowledging the many faces of grief and giving yourself permission to feel, you create space for healing and resilience.

In the following chapters, we will delve into practical strategies for navigating the practical and emotional adjustments that follow the loss of a spouse.

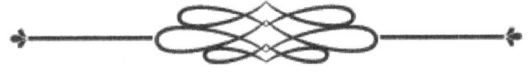

Chapter 4: How Love Shapes Loss

A Unique Grief:

Love and loss are intricately intertwined. The depth of grief we feel when losing a spouse is a reflection of the love we shared with them. In this chapter, we explore how love influences the grieving process and provides both pain and a pathway toward healing.

The Profound Bond of Partnership

Losing a spouse is unlike any other loss because of the unique bond you shared. This relationship is often the foundation of your daily life, providing emotional, physical, and spiritual intimacy. The loss can feel as though a part of your own identity has been torn away.

- **A Shared History:** The memories, milestones, and struggles you navigated together create a tapestry that is now missing its central thread.

- **Emotional Anchors:** Your spouse likely served as a confidant, cheerleader, and source of unconditional support. Their absence can leave you feeling adrift.

- **Future Dreams:** Beyond shared history, love also involves shared visions of the future. The loss of these dreams compounds the pain of grief.

Understanding the depth of this connection helps explain why grief feels so overwhelming. It's not just the absence of a person but the loss of a shared life.

The Pain of Attachment

Attachment is at the core of love. When we form deep connections, our brains and hearts adapt to the presence of our loved ones. The loss of a spouse disrupts these attachments, creating emotional and physiological responses that can feel unbearable.

- **The Physical Heartache:** Studies have shown that grief can manifest as actual pain, often described as a "broken heart." This physical response underscores how deeply love is embedded in our being.

- **Triggers of Loss:** Familiar places, objects, or routines can bring sharp reminders of your spouse's absence. These triggers can evoke intense waves of longing and sorrow.

- **The Need for Connection:** Even in their absence, the bond remains. You might find yourself talking to your spouse, imagining their presence, or seeking comfort in their belongings.

This attachment doesn't fade quickly, nor should it be expected to. It's a testament to the love you shared.

Shared Histories

While love amplifies the pain of loss, it also offers a wellspring of strength. The love you shared can become a guiding light in your journey through grief.

- **Cherished Memories:** Reflecting on happy moments with your spouse can bring comfort. These memories are a reminder of the joy and connection you experienced.

- **Lessons Learned:** Your relationship likely shaped your values, perspectives, and resilience. Carrying these lessons forward can be a way of honoring your spouse.

- **Continuing Bonds:** Many grieving individuals find solace in maintaining a connection with their loved one. This might involve rituals, such as lighting a candle, visiting a special place, or speaking to them in your thoughts.

The Transformative Power of Love

Over time, the intense pain of loss can begin to transform. This doesn't mean forgetting or "moving on" but finding a way to integrate your love into your life's new reality.

- **Growth Through Grief:** Grieving the loss of a spouse often deepens your capacity for empathy, compassion, and appreciation for life.

- **Legacy of Love:** Your spouse's influence remains a part of you. Whether through shared tradition, inside jokes, or values they instilled, their presence continues to shape your life.

- **Reopening to Love:** Some people fear that healing might mean betraying their love for their spouse. In truth, healing allows you to honor their memory while remaining open to love in all its forms—be it friendships, family bonds, or even new romantic relationships.

The Loneliness of Absence

When framed through the lens of love, grief becomes more than just pain; it becomes a testament to the profound connection you shared. Allow yourself to feel the full spectrum of your emotions, knowing they arise from a place of deep love.

- **Acceptance of Emotions:** Embrace the sadness, anger, and even moments of joy that come with grief. They are all part of your love's legacy.

- **Honoring Your Spouse:** Find meaningful ways to celebrate their life and the love you shared. This might involve creating a memorial, supporting a cause they cared about, or simply living in a way that reflects their values.

Finding Hope in Love's Endurance

Grief can feel like the end of love, but in truth, love endures in ways that transcend loss. The love you shared with your spouse continues to shape who you are and how you engage with the world. It's a reminder that while life has changed, the impact of their presence in your life remains unshakable. In the next chapter, we will explore the practical and emotional adjustments necessary to rebuild a life after loss, helping you navigate the path forward while honoring the love that remains.

Part 3: Navigating Change and Growth

Chapter 5: Rebuilding a Life After Loss

The loss of a spouse marks a profound turning point. Life as you knew it has changed irrevocably, and rebuilding a sense of normalcy can feel daunting. In this chapter, we focus on the practical and emotional adjustments needed to forge a new path while honoring the past.

Navigating the Practical Realities

CHAPTER 5: REBUILDING A LIFE AFTER LOSS

After losing a spouse, many find themselves overwhelmed by the practical responsibilities that follow. These tasks, though challenging, are necessary steps toward regaining a sense of control and stability.

- **Financial Adjustments:**

  - Review your financial situation, including joint accounts, insurance policies, and debts.

  - Seek guidance from a financial advisor if needed to create a sustainable plan for the future.

- **Household Responsibilities:**

  - Tasks once shared may now fall entirely to you. Establishing routines for chores, maintenance, and caregiving (if applicable) can ease this transition.

- **Legal and Administrative Tasks:**

  - Handle the legal aspects, such as settling the estate, updating beneficiaries, and addressing property ownership. This process can be emotionally taxing, so seek support from professionals or trusted friends if necessary.

Coping with Emotional Adjustments

The emotional landscape after loss is often turbulent, with conflicting feelings emerging as you adjust to your new reality.

- **Rediscovering Independence:**

    - Without your spouse, decisions that were once shared must now be made alone. While intimidating at first, this independence can also lead to personal growth and self-reliance.

- **Allowing Space for Grief:**

    - It's important to honor your feelings and allow grief to unfold naturally. Pushing yourself to "move on" prematurely can hinder healing.

- **Managing Loneliness:**

    - The absence of daily companionship can be particularly painful. Finding ways to connect with others, such as through support groups or social activities, can help mitigate feelings of isolation.

Rediscovering Your Identity

When you lose a spouse, it's not just their presence you grieve—it's also the identity you shared as a couple. Rebuilding your sense of self is a gradual but essential part of moving forward.

- **Exploring New Interests:**

    - Consider hobbies or activities you've always wanted to try. This exploration can be a way to reconnect with yourself and discover new sources of joy.

- **Evaluating Priorities:**

    - Reflect on your goals and values. What matters most to you now? How can you align your life with these priorities?

- **Creating Rituals for Connection:**

    - Many find comfort in developing rituals to honor their spouse's memory, such as visiting a special place, celebrating your wedding anniversary, or supporting causes they cared about.

Finding a New Normal

Support from others is invaluable as you navigate life after loss. Surrounding yourself with understanding and compassionate individuals can ease the burden of grief.

- **Family and Friends:**

  - Lean on your loved ones for emotional and practical support. Share your feelings openly and let them know how they can help. Don't be embarrassed about shedding tears, it's a normal part of the grieving process.

- **Support Groups:**

  - Connecting with others who have experienced similar losses can provide validation and camaraderie. Many communities offer grief support groups specifically for widows and widowers.

- **Professional Guidance:**
  - If grief feels insurmountable, consider seeking help from a therapist or counselor. Professional support can offer tools for coping and insight into your healing process.

Honoring the Journey

Rebuilding after loss is not a linear process. There will be setbacks and moments of doubt, but each step forward—no matter how small—is a testament to your strength and capacity to heal.

In the next chapter, we will explore the power of resilience and how to cultivate hope, even in the face of profound loss.

Chapter 6: Cultivating Resilience and Hope

The journey through grief is neither straightforward nor easy, but it reveals the profound resilience of the human spirit. In this chapter, we explore how to nurture resilience, embrace hope, and find ways to live meaningfully even after profound loss.

What is Resilience?

Resilience is the ability to adapt to adversity and recover from challenges. It doesn't mean avoiding pain or "bouncing back" to the person you were before your loss. Instead, resilience involves integrating the experience of loss into your life and growing through it.

- **Misconceptions About Resilience:**

  - Resilience is not about "being strong" or suppressing emotions. True resilience involves processing and working through grief in healthy ways.

  - It's also not a fixed trait; resilience can be cultivated and strengthened over time.

Building Blocks of Resilience

While the path to resilience looks different for everyone, certain practices and mindsets can support your journey:

1. **Self-Compassion:**

   - Speak to yourself with kindness and understanding, especially on days when grief feels overwhelming.

   - Avoid harsh self-criticism or unrealistic expectations of how you "should" feel or act.

2. **Mindfulness and Presence:**

    ◦ Engage in mindfulness practices to stay grounded in the present moment.

    ◦ Techniques like meditation, deep breathing, or journaling can help you navigate the emotional waves of grief.

3. **Strengthening Social Connections:**

    ◦ Seek out relationships that offer empathy and encouragement.

    ◦ Lean on your support network, and don't hesitate to ask for help when you need it.

4. **Focusing on Small Steps:**

    ◦ Set realistic goals for yourself, even if they're as simple as getting out of bed, preparing a meal, or going for a walk.

    ◦ Celebrate small victories, recognizing them as meaningful progress.

The Role of Hope in Healing

Hope doesn't mean denying your grief or pretending everything is okay. It's about believing that life can hold meaning, joy, and connection again, even in the wake of loss.

- **Finding Hope in Small Moments:**

    - Pay attention to moments of beauty or peace, such as a sunrise, a kind word, or a cherished memory.

    - These glimpses of hope can remind you that life continues to offer experiences worth savoring.

- **Reframing Loss:**

    - Instead of viewing grief as something to "get over," consider it a testament to the depth of your love.

    - Embrace the idea that grief and joy can coexist, allowing you to honor your spouse's memory while finding fulfillment in the present.

Practical Strategies for Cultivating Resilience

Nurturing resilience requires action, reflection, and patience. Below are strategies to help you move toward healing:

- **Develop New Routines:**

    - Establishing routines provides structure and a sense of normalcy amid the chaos of grief.

    - Over time, these routines can become comforting and help anchor your days.

- **Explore Creative Outlets:**

    - Creativity can be a powerful way to process emotions. Activities like painting, writing, music, or crafting can provide an outlet for expression.

    - Consider creating something in memory of your spouse, such as a scrapbook, poem, or garden.

- **Engage in Acts of Service:**

- Helping others can bring a sense of purpose and connection. Volunteering or supporting causes your spouse cared about can be especially meaningful.

- **Prioritize Physical Health:**

  - Regular exercise, a balanced diet, and adequate sleep support your overall well-being and ability to cope with stress.

  - Even small steps, like a daily walk or drinking enough water, can make a difference.

Stories of Resilience

Hearing stories of others who have navigated loss can inspire hope and remind you that healing is possible. Here are a few examples:

- A widow who rediscovered her passion for gardening, finding solace and renewal in nurturing life.

- A widower who joined a local hiking group, forging new friendships and reclaiming his love for the outdoors.

- A mate who started a charity in their loved one's name, transforming their grief into a lasting legacy.

Embracing the Possibility of Joy

As you cultivate resilience, moments of joy may begin to appear. These can feel unexpected or even unsettling initially, but they are a natural part of healing.

- **Permitting Yourself to Feel Joy:**

    - Feeling happiness or laughter doesn't mean you've forgotten your spouse or moved on. It shows your capacity to embrace life while carrying their memory with you.

- **Reconnecting with Passions:**

    - Revisit activities or interests that bring you a sense of fulfillment. These can serve as bridges to a brighter future.

Looking Ahead

Cultivating resilience and hope is not about erasing grief but learning to live with it in a way that honors your love and your life. The journey is deeply personal, and there is no single "right" path. With time, support, and intentionality, you can find your way toward a life reflecting your loss and strength.

In the next chapter, we will explore how to keep your loved one's memory alive while continuing to grow and evolve in your own life.

Chapter 7: Keeping Memories Alive

Grief doesn't end when you reach a particular milestone, nor does the love you have for your spouse. Keeping their memory alive can provide comfort, meaning, and a continued connection as you move forward. This chapter explores ways to honor your loved one, cherish shared memories, and find a balance between remembrance and renewal.

Why We Remember

Memories are more than reflections of the past; they shape how we carry our loved ones into the future. Remembering your spouse is a way to:

- **Celebrate Their Life:** Memories highlight the joy and significance of your time together.

- **Strengthen Connection:** Reflecting on their values, habits, and stories helps keep their essence close.

- **Find Meaning:** Honoring their memory can help you navigate grief by focusing on their impact on your life and others.

Personal Ways to Honor Their Memory

Everyone remembers and honors their loved one differently. These personal acts can serve as a tribute to their life and your bond:

- **Create a Memorial:**

    - Plant a tree or create a garden in their name.

    - Dedicate a bench, plaque, or space that

holds significance to both of you.

- **Celebrate Anniversaries:**

  - Acknowledge essential dates, such as wedding anniversaries, by lighting a candle, sharing a favorite meal with people who knew your spouse, or doing something your spouse enjoyed.

- **Incorporate Their Belongings:**

  - Use their belongings in creative ways, such as quilting pieces of their clothing or framing a handwritten note.

Shared Remembrance with Others

Keeping memories alive can also be a communal act. Sharing stories and creating traditions with family and friends fosters connection and ensures your loved one's legacy endures:

- **Storytelling:**

  - Gather with loved ones to share memories, anecdotes, and lessons from your spouse's life.

- Consider creating a memory book where friends and family can contribute their recollections.

- **Charitable Actions:**

  - Volunteer or donate to causes your spouse cared about, turning your grief into a positive impact.

  - Establish a scholarship, fund, or event in their name.

Balancing Remembrance and Moving Forward

While keeping memories alive is essential, allowing space for new experiences is also essential. The balance between honoring the past and embracing the present is deeply personal:

- **Avoiding Guilt:**

  - Finding joy or moving forward doesn't diminish your love for your spouse. It's a testament to their influence on your resilience.

- **Creating New Memories:**

  - Engage in activities or relationships that bring you fulfillment while cherishing the past. For example, you might form a new circle of friends who live alone, rather than spending all your social events with couples.

- **Adapting Traditions:**

  - Modify shared traditions in ways that feel right for you, blending old and new.

When Remembrance Becomes Overwhelming

Sometimes, the act of remembering can intensify feelings of grief or sadness. It's important to recognize when to step back and seek balance:

- **Setting Boundaries:**

  - Limit exposure to triggers when memories feel too heavy to bear.

- **Seeking Support:**

- Lean on friends, family, or counselors to help process intense emotions tied to remembrance.

- **Allowing Change:**

  - It's okay to shift how you honor your loved one over time. Your methods of remembrance may evolve as you heal. When your loss is new, looking at family photos may bring on bouts of sadness accompanied by uncontrollable weeping. However, as time goes by and you begin the healing process, photos and other shared memories will likely bring a smile to your face as you recall the feelings you shared with your mate.

Living Their Legacy

One of the most profound ways to keep your spouse's memory alive is by living their values and carrying their influence into your life:

- **Embody Their Teachings:**

  - Reflect on lessons your spouse shared and how they shaped your worldview.

Carry these values forward in your actions.

- **Share Their Story:**

  - Keep their memory alive by talking about them openly with those who knew them and introducing their story to new friends. This kind of tribute to your spouse can be a significant part of the healing process.

- **Pursue Their Dreams:**

  - If they had unrealized aspirations or goals, consider pursuing them in their honor, whether traveling to a place they dreamed of or continuing a project they started. For example, traveling to a place they dreamed of is a great way to incorporate the memory of your spouse with new happy experiences.

Embracing a Future Rooted in Love

Keeping memories alive is not about clinging to the past but integrating it into your ongoing story. By honoring your spouse's life and legacy, you can find ways to celebrate their impact while creating a future infused with the love they gave you. However you choose to honor your mate, remember that you will have the opportunity to share it with your spouse when you are reunited with them after they are resurrected. For more information about this, see Chapter 16: The Resurrection Hope

In the next chapter, we will delve into finding meaning after loss, exploring how grief can transform your perspective and inspire new purpose in life.

Chapter 8: Finding Meaning After Loss

As painful as it is, grief can also become a catalyst for personal growth and transformation. While the loss of a spouse leaves an irreplaceable void, it also challenges us to seek new purpose and meaning in life. This chapter explores how to navigate the journey of finding meaning after loss, emphasizing the importance of honoring your spouse's legacy while embracing the future.

Why Meaning Matters

The search for meaning is a fundamental human instinct, especially after a significant loss. Finding meaning doesn't erase grief but provides a framework for understanding and navigating it. Meaning helps:

- **Anchor You in the Present:** It offers a sense of direction amid the chaos of loss.

- **Transform Pain into Purpose:** It allows you to channel your grief into actions and decisions that reflect your values and your loved one's influence.

- **Rebuild Your Identity:** It helps redefine who you are in your spouse's absence, creating space for growth and self-discovery.

The Many Paths to Meaning

Every individual's journey to finding meaning is unique. Below are some common paths that can inspire and guide your exploration:

1. **Embracing Your Loved One's Legacy:**

   - Reflect on the values, passions, and dreams of your spouse. How can you carry those forward in your life?

- Examples: Continuing their charitable work, nurturing shared traditions, or supporting causes they cared about.

2. **Engaging in Personal Growth:**

- Loss often prompts deep reflection about life's priorities and your potential.

- Examples: Pursuing education, developing new skills, or exploring hobbies that bring you joy and fulfillment.

3. **Fostering Connection:**

- Meaning can be found in relationships by strengthening existing bonds or forming new ones.

- Examples: Mentoring others, joining support groups, or deepening connections with family and friends.

4. **Creating and Expressing:**

- Creativity allows you to process emotions and honor your spouse in a deeply personal way.

- Examples: Writing a memoir, painting,

composing music, or crafting something in their memory.

Transforming Grief Into Purpose

Turning grief into purpose doesn't mean avoiding or suppressing your pain. Instead, it involves integrating the experience of loss into your life in ways that bring meaning and hope:

- **Volunteering or Advocacy:**
  - Use your experience to help others going through similar challenges.
  - Example: Advocating for support services for widows and widowers or volunteering at a hospice or counseling center.

- **Rituals and Memorials:**
  - Create traditions or spaces that allow for ongoing remembrance and reflection.
  - Example: Organizing an annual event in your spouse's honor, such as a charity run or community gathering.

- **Pursuing Unfulfilled Dreams:**

    - If your spouse had goals or dreams they couldn't complete, consider how you might fulfill them.

    - Example: Traveling to a place they always wanted to visit or completing a project they were passionate about.

Embracing Change

The journey of finding meaning often requires embracing change—both within yourself and in your circumstances:

- **Reimagining Your Future:**

    - Acknowledge that your life may not look the way you once envisioned, and that's okay. When you are in the initial stages of grief, especially if you are experiencing anger or depression, it can be difficult to imagine that your life will ever be okay again. But as you begin the healing process, your vision of your future will brighten.

- Focus on possibilities for growth, discovery, and joy.

- **Rebuilding Your Identity:**

  - The loss of a spouse often prompts questions about who you are without them. Losing a mate can make you feel damaged and heartbroken, but these feelings won't last forever. As your healing process progresses and your sadness begins to lessen, you will notice that you start referring to yourself as "I" instead of "we".

  - Use this time to explore your interests, values, and aspirations.

- **Allowing Yourself to Grow:**

  - Grief is transformative, reshaping how you see the world and yourself.

  - Give yourself permission to grow and change without feeling like you're leaving your spouse behind.

The Role of Gratitude

Gratitude can play a decisive role in finding meaning after loss. It's not about dismissing your grief but about recognizing the moments of love, beauty, and connection that still exist:

- **Practicing Daily Gratitude:**
    - Reflect on small moments of joy or kindness each day.
    - Example: A supportive conversation, a beautiful sunset, or a cherished memory.
- **Gratitude for Your Spouse:**
    - Acknowledge the gifts your spouse brought to your life and how their presence shaped who you are.

Stories of Transformation

Hearing how others have found meaning after loss can inspire and encourage you on your journey. Consider these examples:

- A widow who started a nonprofit organization in her spouse's name, supporting a cause they both cherished.

- A widower who found solace in writing and published a book about his journey through grief.

- A mate who returned to school and pursued a career inspired by their loved one's passions.

Finding Meaning Is a Process

It's important to remember that finding meaning doesn't happen overnight. It's a gradual process that unfolds over time, often with setbacks and breakthroughs along the way. Be patient with yourself as you explore what gives your life purpose and fulfillment.

Looking Ahead

Finding meaning after loss is not about moving on but about moving forward — carrying the love and memories of your spouse as you build a life that reflects their impact and your resilience. In the next chapter, we will discuss how to approach life's uncertainties with grace and confidence, preparing for a future filled with challenges and possibilities.

Chapter 9: Approaching Uncertainty with Grace

The loss of a spouse disrupts the foundation of your life, leaving you to navigate a future filled with uncertainty. Questions about your purpose, relationships, and day-to-day existence can feel overwhelming. However, learning to face life's unpredictability with grace can empower you to embrace the unknown and find a sense of peace amid the chaos. This chapter explores strategies for managing uncertainty, building resilience, and cultivating hope for the future.

Understanding the Nature of Uncertainty

Uncertainty is an inherent part of life, but after a profound loss, it can feel particularly unsettling and overwhelming. Recognizing its role and accepting that it's a natural aspect of the human experience is a vital first step:

- **The Unknown Is Inevitable:** No one has a clear map of their future; life unfolds in ways we cannot always predict or control.

- **Loss Amplifies Uncertainty:** The death of a spouse often magnifies the unknown, forcing you to confront questions about identity, stability, and purpose. In addition to that, there may be routine tasks that your spouse used to take care of that you are now dealing with for the first time. For example, did your mate manage the monthly expenses and pay all the bills? Or perhaps your spouse tended to your lawn and garden. My husband was an electrician so I never had to learn how to open light fixtures to change light bulbs. The first time I had to use a step stool and figure out how to open the entryway light fixture, it left me sobbing uncontrollably. But as the years went by, I've learned to master this mundane task.

- **Opportunity Within Ambiguity:** Although uncertainty can feel daunting, even overwhelming, it also holds the potential for discovery and growth.

Building Resilience in the Face of Uncertainty

Resilience is your ability to adapt and thrive despite challenges. (For more about resilience see Chapter 6: Cultivating Resilience and Hope) Cultivating resilience helps you manage uncertainty with confidence and strength:

1. **Focus on What You Can Control:**

    ◦ Direct your energy toward areas where you can make a difference, such as self-care, setting goals, and maintaining routines.

2. **Cultivate a Flexible Mindset:**

    ◦ Be open to change and new possibilities. Flexibility allows you to adjust to unexpected developments and approach them with curiosity rather than fear.

3. **Practice Self-Compassion:**

   - Acknowledge your feelings without judgment. Give yourself grace as you navigate difficult emotions and transitions.

4. **Seek Out Support:**

   - Lean on friends, family, or professional counselors. Sharing your concerns can lighten the burden of uncertainty and provide valuable perspective.

Navigating Key Areas of Uncertainty

After losing a spouse, you may face uncertainty in several specific areas of life. Addressing these directly can help you regain a sense of stability and purpose:

1. **Financial Security:**

   - Review your financial situation, seeking professional advice if necessary. Understanding your resources and options can alleviate anxiety about your financial future.

2. **Family Dynamics:**

- Relationships with children, in-laws, and extended family may shift after your loss. Open communication and setting boundaries are key to maintaining healthy connections.

3. **Social Connections:**

- Social circles often change after a loss. Be intentional about nurturing existing friendships and exploring opportunities to meet new people who share your interests or experiences.

4. **Redefining Roles:**

- The roles you shared with your spouse—as a caregiver, decision-maker, and partner—will undoubtedly require adjustment. Reflect on how you can adapt to new responsibilities with confidence.

Strategies for Embracing the Unknown

Instead of resisting uncertainty, learning to embrace it can help you find strength and meaning in life's unpredictability:

1. **Stay Present:**

    - Focus on the present moment rather than worrying about the unknown future. Mindfulness practices like meditation, deep breathing, or journaling can help ground you.

2. **Set Small Goals:**

    - Break down overwhelming challenges into manageable steps. Achieving small milestones builds confidence and creates momentum. For example, use a daily or weekly "To-Do" list. As you complete each task, cross it off the list. You'll be surprised how this simple activity will give you a sense of accomplishment and a feeling of control over your life. One more thing, don't throw those completed lists away. Save them in a drawer or notebook and on days that you are feeling overwhelmed or depressed, take a look at those lists and reflect on how far you have come.

3. **Welcome New Experiences:**

- Trying new activities or pursuing interests can open doors to opportunities and relationships you might not have considered before. These new relationships could be building new friendships or as time goes on, you may even consider a new romantic relationship. The healing process is a uniquely individual experience. Try not to engage in self-judgment regarding the possibility of a new romantic relationship.

4. **Trust in Your Resilience:**

- Remind yourself of past challenges you've overcome. Journaling is a good way to keep track of your emotional growth and accomplishments over time. Your capacity to adapt and endure is greater than you may realize.

Finding Hope Amid Uncertainty

Hope is the anchor that sustains you through the storm of grief and uncertainty. Nurturing hope doesn't mean denying the reality of your loss; it means believing in the possibility of joy and meaning again:

- **Allow Hope to Emerge Gradually:**

  - Hope may feel distant at first, but it grows through small moments of connection, accomplishment, and peace.

- **Seek Inspiration:**

  - Stories of others who have rebuilt their lives after loss can provide encouragement and motivation. Joining a grief support group might seem too painful to contemplate or unnecessary when your loss is new. As time goes on and your healing begins, you may feel differently about the opportunity. Over the months and years revisit your decision as you reflect on your progress.

- **Hold Space for Possibility:**

  - Even if the future feels unclear, trust that it holds potential for healing and fulfillment.

Lessons from Uncertainty

Facing uncertainty teaches profound lessons about resilience, acceptance, and the human capacity for growth:

- **The Value of Adaptability:**

  - Life rarely follows a straight path, and learning to adapt is essential for moving forward.

- **The Strength in Vulnerability:**

  - Acknowledging your fears and uncertainties can be a source of courage and connection with others.

- **The Gift of Perspective:**

  - Uncertainty can help you appreciate the present moment and the people and experiences that bring meaning to your life.

Looking Forward with Grace

Navigating uncertainty with grace is not about having all the answers but about cultivating the courage to face life's unknowns with hope and resilience. By focusing on what you can control, embracing change, and trusting in your ability to grow, you can find peace in the midst of unpredictability.

In the next chapter, we will explore how to cultivate joy and fulfillment again, offering strategies for rediscovering happiness and purpose as you move forward on your journey.

Chapter 10: Rediscovering Joy and Purpose

Grief, while deeply painful, is not the end of your story. Within the shadow of loss lies the opportunity to rediscover joy and a renewed sense of purpose. Rebuilding a fulfilling life after the death of a spouse is a gradual process, one that honors your past while embracing the future. This chapter offers practical guidance for reclaiming happiness and finding meaningful purpose as you move forward.

Understanding Joy After Loss

Joy might feel distant or even impossible after profound loss, but it is not out of reach. The return of joy does not diminish the love or memory of your spouse; instead, it is a testament to the resilience of the human spirit:

- **Grief and Joy Can Coexist:** The ability to experience happiness does not mean your grief has ended. You carry both, allowing moments of joy to shine through even in sorrow.

- **Joy Is Found in the Present:** Joy often arises unexpectedly in small, simple moments—a shared laugh, a comforting memory, or an act of kindness. Initially, experiencing joy or laughter may bring with it feelings of guilt, as if experiencing joy without your spouse is somehow disloyal to their memory.

- **Reclaiming Joy Is an Act of Strength:** By allowing yourself to experience happiness, you honor your capacity to heal and grow.

Steps to Rediscover Joy

Acknowledge Small Pleasures:

Pay attention to the small moments of beauty and happiness in daily life, such as a sunrise, a favorite song, or the taste of a good meal. The Psalmist speaks about how numerous God's wonderful works are:

Many, Lord my God,
are the wonders you have done,
the things you planned for us.
None can compare with you;
were I to speak and tell of your deeds,
they would be too many to declare. (Psalms 40:5, NIV)

Engage in Activities That Bring Fulfillment:

1. Reconnect with hobbies, interests, or creative pursuits you may have set aside. These activities can rekindle a sense of joy and accomplishment.

2. **Surround Yourself with Positivity:**

    - Seek out people and environments that uplift and support you. Spending time with loved ones or joining new social groups can be a source of comfort and connection.

3. **Practice Gratitude:**

   - Reflect on the aspects of your life that bring meaning and contentment. Keeping a gratitude journal can help shift your focus toward positivity.

Defining a New Sense of Purpose

Losing your spouse may leave you questioning your purpose. This is true because often much of our identity stems from the roles we played in partnership with our mate; such as caregiver, and confidant. Rediscovering purpose involves finding what gives your life meaning and direction in this new chapter:

- **Honor Your Spouse's Influence:**

  - Consider how their values, dreams, or legacy might inspire you to take meaningful action in your life.

- **Explore Your Passions:**

- Reflect on your own interests and goals. What activities, causes, or roles ignite a sense of fulfillment and pride?

- **Set Intentional Goals:**

  - Purpose grows from having a clear direction. Start with small, achievable goals that align with your values and expand over time.

Reconnecting with Others

Relationships play a crucial role in rediscovering joy and purpose. Rebuilding and expanding your social connections can help you feel supported and valued:

1. **Strengthen Existing Bonds:**

   - Spend time with friends and family who provide comfort and encouragement. Shared experiences can be a source of healing.

2. **Form New Connections:**

   - Join community groups, attend events, or

volunteer for causes that resonate with you. Meeting people with similar interests or experiences can foster meaningful relationships.

3. **Give Back to Others:**

    - Helping others can bring profound fulfillment. Whether through volunteering, mentoring, or acts of kindness, contributing to the well-being of others reinforces your sense of purpose.

Balancing Reflection and Forward Movement

As you rediscover joy and purpose, balance the act of honoring your past with embracing the future:

- **Celebrate Your Spouse's Legacy:**

    - Create rituals or traditions that keep their memory alive while allowing space for your own growth.

- **Allow Yourself to Evolve:**

    - Grief transforms you in profound ways.

Embrace the person you are becoming, even as you cherish the love that shaped you.

- **Be Patient with Yourself:**

    - Rediscovering joy and purpose is a journey, not a destination. Allow time for setbacks and celebrate progress, no matter how small.

Signs of Renewal

As you move through this process, you may notice signs that you are beginning to rediscover joy and purpose:

- **Increased Energy and Optimism:**

    - You feel more willing to engage in activities and look forward to the future.

- **A Sense of Gratitude:**

    - You find yourself appreciating the people, experiences, and opportunities that enrich your life.

- **Moments of Peace:**

- Though grief remains, it no longer dominates every thought or experience.

Stories of Renewal

Hearing how others have reclaimed their lives after loss can inspire hope and direction. Consider these examples:

- A widow who started a community garden in her spouse's memory, fostering connection and growth.

- A man who turned to painting as a way to process grief and found a new passion that brought him joy and recognition.

- A mate who volunteered at an animal shelter, finding solace and purpose through caring for others.

Looking Forward with Hope

Rediscovering joy and purpose is a testament to your resilience and capacity for growth. It is not about forgetting your loss but about finding ways to live fully while carrying the love and memories of your spouse with you. As you take steps to embrace happiness and meaning, you pave the way for a future filled with possibilities.

Chapter 11: Rediscovering Your Identity

Losing a spouse is not only the loss of a beloved companion but also a disruption to your own sense of self. For years, perhaps decades, your identity was intertwined with theirs. Together, you built a life, shared dreams, and created routines. You were not just you but part of a "we." When that "we" is shattered by loss, it can leave you questioning who you are and what your life looks like moving forward. Rediscovering your identity after such a profound loss is a journey—a process of understanding, redefining, and embracing the person you are becoming.

The Void Left Behind

The loss of a spouse can bring about a deep sense of disorientation. Roles and responsibilities that were once shared may now fall entirely on your shoulders. If you were primarily a caregiver, a partner in decision-making, or someone who depended on your spouse for certain aspects of life, their absence might leave you feeling unmoored. You may also find that some aspects of your personality or interests were expressed more fully in the context of your relationship. Now, without them, it can feel like parts of you are missing too.

This sense of loss is not unusual. It's a natural part of grieving and adjusting to life without your spouse. The key is to acknowledge these feelings while gently beginning the process of rediscovering who you are, both as an individual and as someone shaped by the love you shared.

Allowing Yourself to Mourn the Changes

Before you can rediscover your identity, it's important to honor what was lost. Mourning is not just about grieving your spouse; it's also about grieving the version of yourself that existed within your relationship. This might include the roles you played, the plans you had, and the future you envisioned together. Give yourself permission to feel the sadness, confusion, and even fear that comes with these changes.

You might find it helpful to journal about the roles you played in your relationship and how they have changed. Write about the parts of your identity that feel most affected by your loss. These reflections can help you process your emotions and begin to identify the areas where you may need to rebuild.

Re-evaluating Your Roles

One of the first steps in rediscovering your identity is reassessing the roles and responsibilities you now hold. These might include practical tasks, such as managing finances or household duties that your spouse once handled. It can also mean navigating new social dynamics, such as attending events alone or redefining relationships with mutual friends and family.

While these adjustments can be daunting, they also provide opportunities for growth. Taking on new responsibilities may reveal strengths and capabilities you didn't realize you had. As you grow more confident in these areas, you'll begin to see yourself in a new light—as someone resilient, resourceful, and capable of navigating life's challenges.

Reconnecting with Your Passions

Grief has a way of narrowing our focus. In the early days, it's hard to think about anything beyond the pain of loss. But as time goes on, you may find yourself longing for activities or interests that once brought you joy. Reconnecting with these passions can be a powerful way to rediscover your identity.

Think about hobbies, talents, or aspirations that were important to you before or during your relationship. Did you love painting, writing, gardening, or traveling? Were there dreams you put on hold because life took you in a different direction? Now may be the time to revisit these pursuits. They can provide not only a sense of purpose but also a way to celebrate the person you are becoming.

Exploring New Possibilities

Rediscovering your identity is not just about reconnecting with the past; it's also about exploring new possibilities. Grief changes us, often in profound ways. As you navigate life without your spouse, you may find that your interests, priorities, and even values have shifted. This is a natural part of growth and healing.

Consider trying something completely new. Take a class, join a club, or volunteer for a cause that resonates with you. Stepping outside your comfort zone can be intimidating, but it can also be incredibly rewarding. These experiences can help you discover new passions and build confidence in your ability to adapt and thrive.

Honoring Your Spouse While Embracing Yourself

Rediscovering your identity does not mean leaving your spouse's memory behind. In fact, their influence will always be a part of who you are. The love you shared, the lessons they taught you, and the life you built together have shaped you in countless ways.

Find ways to honor their memory as you embrace your new identity. This might include continuing traditions they cherished, creating a memorial project, or simply carrying their values forward in your own life. By doing so, you can keep their presence alive while also allowing yourself the freedom to grow and change.

The Role of Faith in Rediscovery

For many, faith plays a central role in the process of rediscovering identity. Turning to God for guidance and strength can provide clarity and peace as you navigate this journey. The Bible reminds us that our identity is ultimately rooted in our relationship with God. As 2 Corinthians 5:17 says, *"Therefore, if anyone is in Christ, the new creation has come: The old has gone, the new is here!"(NIV)*

Lean into this truth as you explore who you are becoming. Through prayer, reflection, and fellowship, you can find reassurance that your identity is secure in God's love, even as it transforms through life's changes.

Steps Toward Rediscovery

Reflect on Your Strengths: Make a list of qualities and skills that have helped you navigate life so far.

Celebrate these strengths and consider how they can guide you in this new chapter.

Set Small Goals: Start with manageable steps to explore your interests or take on new responsibilities. Each accomplishment will build your confidence and sense of self.

Seek Support: Surround yourself with people who encourage and affirm you. Share your journey with trusted friends, family, or a support group.

Give Yourself Compassion: Rediscovery takes time. Be patient with yourself and acknowledge that growth often comes in small, gradual steps.

A New Chapter Begins

Rediscovering your identity after loss is not about becoming someone entirely new; it's about uncovering the person you are now—a person shaped by love, resilience, and hope. As you take steps toward embracing this new chapter, remember that you carry the essence of your spouse's love and influence with you. They remain a part of your story, even as you continue to write new pages.

Chapter 12: Building Self-Confidence After a Loss

The loss of a spouse can profoundly shake your self-confidence. For years, your identity and confidence may have been intertwined with your role in the relationship. Together, you faced challenges, celebrated victories, and found strength in each other. When your mate is gone, it's natural to feel unsure of yourself, questioning your ability to move forward independently.

Yet, the Bible reminds us that we are not alone even in the most challenging times. God is our source of strength and guidance, equipping us to rebuild and flourish after loss. This chapter explores the journey of rebuilding self-confidence, offering practical steps and spiritual encouragement to navigate this process with faith and resilience.

The Impact of Loss on Self-Confidence

Losing a spouse often brings a sense of disorientation. Your shared roles and routines shift, leaving you to navigate life alone. Simple tasks, like managing finances or making decisions, can feel overwhelming. You may even question your worth, wondering how to function without the validation and partnership you once enjoyed.

This loss of confidence is not a reflection of weakness but a natural response to a significant life change. Recognizing this is the first step toward healing.

Biblical Encouragement for Strength and Courage

The Bible offers a wealth of wisdom and comfort for those who feel unsteady after a loss. One of the most reassuring passages comes from the book of Joshua, where God encourages Joshua to take on a leadership role after Moses' death:

"Have I not commanded you? Be strong and courageous. Do not be afraid; do not be discouraged, for the Lord your God will be with you wherever you go." (Joshua 1:9, NIV)

This verse underscores the promise that God's presence is constant, even when we feel most vulnerable. Just as God was with Joshua as he faced an uncertain future, He is with you now, providing the courage to rebuild your life.

Steps to Rebuild Self-Confidence

Rebuilding self-confidence is a process that requires patience, intentionality, and faith. Below are practical steps to help you rediscover your sense of self and regain confidence.

1. Reflect on Your Strengths and Accomplishments

CHAPTER 12: BUILDING SELF-CONFIDENCE AF...

Grief can cloud your memory of past achievements and diminish your sense of worth. Take time to reflect on moments when you overcame challenges or succeeded in tasks. Make a list of your strengths and remind yourself of your capabilities.

The Apostle Paul offers a reminder of God's role in our abilities:

"I can do all this through him who gives me strength." (Philippians 4:13, NIV)

Your accomplishments, both big and small, are a testament to the strength God has already given you. Let this reflection inspire confidence as you face new challenges.

2. Set Small, Achievable Goals

Grief can make even routine tasks feel daunting. Start by setting small, achievable goals to regain a sense of accomplishment. For instance, focus on organizing a part of your home, writing a letter to a loved one, or learning a new skill.

Each success, no matter how minor it seems, contributes to a growing sense of capability. As Jesus said:

"Whoever can be trusted with very little can also be trusted with much." (Luke 16:10, NIV)

Small victories lay the foundation for tackling larger challenges over time.

3. Learn Something New

One of the most empowering ways to build confidence is by acquiring new skills or knowledge. Whether it's learning to cook a new recipe, mastering a hobby, or even pursuing formal education, the process of learning reinforces your ability to adapt and grow.

Ecclesiastes reminds us that there is a time for everything, including growth and renewal:

"There is a time for everything, and a season for every activity under the heavens." (Ecclesiastes 3:1, NIV)

This season of loss can also be a time of discovery and self-reinvention.

4. Connect with Supportive Communities

Isolation can erode self-confidence, while connection fosters growth and resilience. Seek out communities where you feel supported and valued. This could include faith-based groups, grief support networks, or social clubs centered on shared interests.

Proverbs highlights the importance of community:

"As iron sharpens iron, so one person sharpens another." (Proverbs 27:17, NIV)

Through relationships, you can draw strength from others while also contributing your own unique gifts and experiences.

5. Focus on God's View of You

Human grief often leads to self-doubt, but God sees your potential and worth, even when you struggle to see it yourself. The psalmist reminds us of how intimately God knows and values us:

"I praise you because I am fearfully and wonderfully made; your works are wonderful, I know that full well." (Psalms 139:14, NIV)

Meditate on this truth to rebuild your sense of worth and identity in God's eyes.

Addressing Fear and Anxiety

Fear and anxiety often accompany a loss of confidence. You may worry about the future or fear making mistakes. The Bible consistently reassures us that fear is not from God:

"For the Spirit God gave us does not make us timid, but gives us power, love, and self-discipline." (2 Timothy 1:7, NIV)

Combat fear by leaning on God's promises, seeking His guidance through prayer, and trusting in His promises for the future.

Celebrating Progress

As you take steps to rebuild confidence, celebrate your progress. Each step forward is a testament to your resilience and God's faithfulness. The journey may not be linear, but every moment of growth is worth acknowledging.

James encourages us to persevere through trials, knowing they shape and strengthen us:

"Consider it pure joy, my brothers and sisters, whenever you face trials of many kinds, because you know that the testing of your faith produces perseverance." (James 1:2-3, NIV)

Your grief, while painful, can become a source of growth and renewed strength.

Conclusion: Confidence Rooted in Faith

Rebuilding self-confidence after the loss of a spouse is not just about finding independence; it's about rediscovering the strength that comes from trusting in God. The journey requires courage, but you are not alone with each step.

As you reflect on your abilities, set goals, and rely on God's promises, you will find that confidence grows naturally. This confidence is not solely based on personal accomplishments but on the assurance that God is guiding your path and equipping you for the road ahead.

"So we say with confidence, 'The Lord is my helper; I will not be afraid. What can mere mortals do to me?'" (Hebrews 13:6, NIV)

With God as your helper, you can face the future with courage and a renewed sense of purpose. Self-confidence rooted in faith is a lasting foundation, enabling you to navigate life's challenges with grace and strength.

Chapter 13: The Role of Gratitude in Healing

Grief and gratitude might seem like opposite ends of the emotional spectrum, but they are intricately connected in the healing process. After the loss of a mate, it can feel impossible to find anything to be grateful for amid the heartbreak. Yet, as time passes and the sharp edges of grief begin to soften, many find that practicing gratitude becomes essential for coping, growing, and rediscovering joy. In this chapter, we'll explore how gratitude can coexist with sorrow, its transformative power, and practical ways to incorporate it into daily life.

The Paradox of Gratitude in Grief

When you're in the depths of grief, the idea of being grateful can feel out of reach. How can gratitude possibly exist when the love of your life is gone? The paradox is that grief and gratitude are not mutually exclusive; instead, they can enrich and balance each other. Grief acknowledges the pain of loss, while gratitude recognizes the blessings that remain. Both emotions honor the depth of your love and the significance of your journey.

Gratitude doesn't diminish your grief or invalidate your pain. Instead, it provides a lens through which you can begin to see moments of light even in the darkest times. By focusing on the things you're thankful for—the love you shared, the memories you treasure, the support of others—you can start to shift your perspective from one of pure loss to one that includes hope and resilience.

How Gratitude Heals

The healing power of gratitude lies in its ability to reshape your mindset. The Apostle Paul spoke about the transformative power of changing our mindset in Romans 12:2, *"Do not conform to the pattern of this world, but be transformed by the renewing of your mind. Then you will be able to test and approve what God's will is—his good, pleasing and perfect will.(NIV)*

Practicing gratitude can reduce stress, improve mental health, and increase overall well-being. For those grieving a spouse, it offers a way to navigate the emotional turbulence of loss by fostering a sense of connection, purpose, and balance.

Focusing on the Positive: Gratitude helps you recognize the good things in your life, even when you're overwhelmed by sadness. This doesn't mean ignoring your pain but balancing it with an acknowledgment of what brings comfort and meaning. The Bible encourages focusing on the positive things in life at Philippians 4:8, *"Finally, brothers and sisters, whatever is true, whatever is noble, whatever is right, whatever is pure, whatever is lovely, whatever is admirable—if anything is excellent or praiseworthy—think about such things". (NIV)*

Strengthening Relationships: Expressing gratitude can deepen your connections with others. Whether it's thanking a friend for their support or sharing cherished memories of your spouse, gratitude fosters emotional intimacy and mutual understanding.

Promoting Resilience: Gratitude encourages you to see challenges as opportunities for growth. It helps you reframe adversity, focusing on the lessons learned and the strengths developed through your loss.

Finding Gratitude in Shared Love

One of the most profound sources of gratitude in grief is the love you shared with your spouse. Though their physical presence is gone, the bond you created remains an integral part of your life. Reflecting on this love can bring a sense of peace and fulfillment, even as you mourn their absence.

Cherishing the Memories: Every shared moment, from the mundane to the extraordinary, is a gift. By focusing on the joy of these experiences, you honor your spouse's place in your heart and keep their spirit alive.

Appreciating the Lessons Learned: Your spouse likely influenced your life in countless ways, shaping your values, perspectives, and passions. Recognizing and embracing these contributions can be a powerful source of gratitude.

Celebrating the Impact: The love you shared extends beyond your relationship. It has touched family, friends, and the community. Acknowledging this ripple effect can provide comfort and a sense of purpose.

Practical Ways to Cultivate Gratitude

Cultivating gratitude is an active process that requires intention and practice. Here are some practical strategies to help you develop a mindset of thankfulness:

Gratitude Journaling: Write down three things you're grateful for each day. These can be big or small—a kind word from a friend, a beautiful sunset, or a fond memory of your spouse. Over time, this practice can shift your focus from loss to abundance.

Mindfulness Meditation: Spend a few minutes each day reflecting on the positive aspects of your life. Focus on your breath, quiet your mind, and let feelings of peace and gratitude arise naturally.

Expressing Thanks: Take the time to thank the people who have supported you through your grief. A heartfelt note, a simple phone call, or a warm hug can strengthen your connections and uplift your spirit.

The Apostle Paul spoke about the power of expressing thanksgiving to God in prayer: *"Do not be anxious about anything, but in every situation, by prayer and petition, with thanksgiving, present your requests to God. 7 And the peace of God, which transcends all understanding, will guard your hearts and your minds in Christ Jesus." (Philippians 4:6, 7; NIV)*

Creating Rituals of Remembrance: Incorporate gratitude into your rituals for honoring your spouse. Display pictures of your mate, say a prayer, or share a favorite memory with loved ones. These acts of remembrance can be both grounding and healing.

Serving Others: Giving back to others can be a profound way to cultivate gratitude. Volunteer for a cause your spouse cared about or lend a helping hand to someone in need. Acts of kindness create a sense of connection and purpose.

Gratitude as a Bridge to Healing

In the early stages of grief, gratitude might feel distant or even impossible. But as you begin to incorporate it into your life, you may find that it becomes a bridge to healing. Gratitude doesn't erase your pain, but it can coexist with it, offering moments of solace and perspective.

Over time, gratitude can transform how you view your loss. Instead of focusing solely on what you no longer have, you can begin to appreciate what remains—the memories, the lessons, and the love that continues to shape your life.

Faith and Gratitude

For those who lean on faith during times of grief, gratitude takes on an even deeper meaning. The Bible encourages us to give thanks in all circumstances, as recorded in 1 Thessalonians 5:18, *"Give thanks in all circumstances; for this is God's will for you in Christ Jesus."*

Gratitude in faith is not about denying pain or pretending everything is fine. Instead, it's about trusting that God's love and forgiveness are present, even in the midst of sorrow. You can find strength, hope, and a renewed sense of purpose by focusing on His blessings.

The Ripple Effect of Gratitude

Gratitude is contagious. When you practice thankfulness, it not only transforms your own heart but also inspires those around you. By sharing your gratitude with others, you create a ripple effect that spreads hope and positivity. This can be particularly meaningful as you navigate life without your spouse, offering a way to honor their memory while enriching the lives of those around you.

A Journey Toward Wholeness

Gratitude is not a quick fix or a cure for grief. It's a practice—a daily commitment to seeking light in the darkness. As you continue your journey, let gratitude be a guide, helping you navigate the complexities of loss with grace and resilience.

Through gratitude, you can begin to rebuild a life that honors the love you've lost while embracing the possibilities of the future. It's a journey toward wholeness, one step at a time, with gratitude lighting the way.

Chapter 14: Finding Purpose Anew

The loss of a spouse is not just the loss of a loved one; it can also feel like the loss of identity, direction, and purpose. When you have spent years, perhaps decades, building a life together, their absence leaves a void that touches every aspect of your existence. Reclaiming purpose is one of the most challenging yet transformative aspects of the grief journey. This chapter explores how to navigate the search for meaning, redefine your sense of self, and embrace the possibilities of a future filled with renewed purpose.

Understanding the Void

When a spouse passes away, the roles and responsibilities you once shared may shift dramatically. Whether you were a caregiver, a partner in decision-making, or simply someone who looked forward to sharing everyday moments, these roles became disoriented. This loss often brings questions like, "Who am I now?" or "What is my life without them?"

Acknowledging the depth of this void is the first step toward healing. It's natural to feel lost, aimless, or overwhelmed by the absence of your spouse. Rather than pushing these feelings away, allow yourself to sit with them, recognizing that the emptiness is a testament to the life you built together and the love you shared.

Purpose in the Midst of Grief

Grief itself can be a teacher, revealing truths about what matters most in life. While the pain of loss can feel all-consuming, it can also serve as a catalyst for reflection and growth. Finding purpose during grief doesn't mean rushing to "fix" your pain or pretending it isn't there. Instead, it's about seeking meaning amid the sorrow and discovering how to carry your spouse's legacy forward.

Redefining Your Identity: After the loss of a spouse, you may struggle to understand who you are outside the context of your relationship. Begin by exploring your values, passions, and interests. What brings you a sense of fulfillment? What causes or activities ignite your spirit? Rediscovering yourself is an integral part of finding purpose.

Honoring Their Memory: Many find purpose in honoring their spouse's memory. This could involve continuing their work, supporting a cause they cared about, or creating something that reflects their spirit. These actions allow you to keep their presence alive in your life while channeling your love into something meaningful.

Engaging with Others: Isolation can deepen the sense of purposelessness. By connecting with others—whether through community service, support groups, or shared hobbies—you open yourself to new relationships and opportunities to give back. Helping others often becomes a profound source of purpose.

Embracing Change

Change can be daunting, especially when it's forced upon you by loss. Yet, life after loss is inherently about adaptation. As you work through your grief, you may begin to see that change, while painful, also holds the potential for growth.

Small Steps Toward Transformation: Purpose doesn't emerge overnight. It often begins with small steps—trying a new activity, reconnecting with old friends, or setting a modest goal. These incremental changes can create momentum, gradually shifting your focus from what was to what could be.

Learning New Skills: Many widowed individuals find empowerment in learning something new—whether it's taking up painting, learning a language, or pursuing a long-held dream. These endeavors not only fill time but also cultivate a sense of achievement and self-discovery.

Welcoming the Unexpected: Purpose may arise in surprising ways. Stay open to opportunities you hadn't considered before, trusting that life can unfold in beautiful and unexpected directions, even after loss.

The Role of Faith in Rediscovering Purpose

For those who turn to their faith during times of grief, scriptural teachings can provide profound guidance on the search for purpose. The Bible emphasizes the idea that life, even in its most painful moments, has meaning. We are created in the image of God and, therefore, have a conscience, a spiritual yearning, an innate sense of justice, and the capacity to give and receive love. We find this truth in Genesis 1:27, *"So God created mankind in his own image, in the image of God he created them; male and female he created them.* (Romans 2:15, Matthew 5:3, Colossians 3:14)

Living Out Your Spouse's Values: Faith often inspires individuals to live in a way that reflects the values and virtues of their loved ones. Whether through acts of service, kindness, or devotion, carrying forward these values can bring a sense of purpose and continuity.

Drawing Strength from Scripture: Passages such as Jeremiah 29:11 *("For I know the plans I have for you, declares the Lord, plans to prosper you and not to harm you, plans to give you hope and a future")* remind us that even in our darkest moments, there is hope and a future to embrace. (See chapter 17: The Resurrection Hope)

Purpose Through Service

One of the most powerful ways to rediscover purpose is through service to others. Grief can make you acutely aware of the struggles others face, creating a deep well of empathy and compassion. Many find that giving back not only honors their spouse's memory but also brings fulfillment and connection.

Volunteering: Whether it's at a local shelter, hospital, or community center, volunteering allows you to make a tangible difference in the lives of others. It can also provide structure and a sense of accomplishment.

Mentorship: Sharing your experiences with those going through similar losses can be incredibly healing. By offering guidance and support, you transform your pain into a source of strength for others.

Creative Projects: Some choose to channel their grief into creative expressions, such as writing a memoir, creating art, or starting a foundation. These projects can leave a lasting impact while giving your life a renewed sense of purpose.

Finding Joy Again

Rediscovering purpose isn't just about finding meaning; it's also about finding joy. Joy may feel elusive in the aftermath of loss, but it's an essential part of the healing process. Purpose and joy often go hand in hand, each reinforcing the other.

Reclaiming Hobbies: Think about the activities you once loved but may have set aside during your grief. Whether it's gardening, dancing, or traveling, these pursuits can rekindle a sense of happiness and fulfillment.

Creating New Traditions: As you move forward, consider establishing new traditions that reflect your evolving life. These rituals can provide comfort, stability, and a sense of continuity.

Celebrating Small Wins: Recognize and celebrate the moments when you feel a spark of joy or accomplishment. These moments are milestones on your journey toward a purposeful life.

The Legacy of Love

At its core, finding purpose after loss is about carrying forward the love you shared. Your spouse's influence is woven into the fabric of your being, and their legacy lives on through your actions, choices, and relationships.

A Continuing Bond: Many grieving individuals find solace in the concept of a continuing bond with their loved one. This bond doesn't diminish over time but evolves as you grow and change. It's a source of strength, guiding you as you navigate life without them.

Inspiring Others: Your journey toward purpose can inspire those around you. You honor your spouse's memory while uplifting others by demonstrating resilience, hope, and a commitment to living fully.

Building a Life That Reflects Their Love: As you find purpose anew, you create a life that embodies the values, dreams, and love you shared. This is their legacy—a testament to their profound impact on your life.

A Journey Toward Renewal

Finding purpose after the loss of a spouse is not a linear process. It's a journey filled with twists, turns, and moments of doubt. Yet, it's also a journey of discovery, growth, and transformation. By embracing change, seeking meaning, and honoring your loved one's legacy, you can build a life deeply rooted in the past and open to the future.

This renewed sense of purpose doesn't erase your grief but gives it context and direction. It allows you to move forward with intention, carrying the love you've lost while embracing the possibilities that lie ahead. Purpose is not just about finding something to do; it's about rediscovering who you are and what makes your life meaningful. And in this discovery, you see not just healing but hope.

Chapter 15: What Happens at Death? A Biblical Perspective

Death is a universal human experience, yet it remains one of the most profound and mysterious aspects of existence. Across cultures and beliefs, people grapple with questions about what happens after death. The Scriptures offer clear and comforting guidance for those who turn to the Bible. This chapter explores the biblical understanding of death, dispelling common misconceptions while providing hope rooted in God's promises.

The Origin of Death

The Bible explains that death entered the world as a consequence of sin. In the Garden of Eden, Adam and Eve were created perfect, with the prospect of everlasting life. However, their disobedience to God introduced sin into humanity, and with it came death. God's words to Adam illustrate this reality:

"By the sweat of your brow you will eat your food until you return to the ground, since from it you were taken; for dust you are and to dust you will return" (Genesis 3:19, NIV).

This verse underscores the temporary nature of human life. We are made from the dust of the earth, and in death, our physical bodies return to it. Death is not a transition to another plane of consciousness or a continuation of life in another form but rather a cessation of existence as we know it.

The Condition of the Dead

The Bible describes the state of the dead as one of unconsciousness, likening it to sleep. This imagery highlights the absence of awareness, activity, or suffering in death. The book of Ecclesiastes provides a succinct explanation:

"For the living know that they will die, but the dead know nothing; they have no further reward, and even their name is forgotten... Whatever your hand finds to do, do it with all your might, for in the realm of the dead, where you are going, there is neither working nor planning nor knowledge nor wisdom" (Ecclesiastes 9:5, 10, NIV).

These verses clarify that death is a state of inactivity and unconsciousness. The dead are not observing the living, engaging in activities, or existing in another form elsewhere. This understanding can bring comfort by eliminating fears of the unknown or misconceptions about torment or punishment after death.

Trust in God, Not in Humanity

Another important aspect of biblical teaching about death is the futility of relying on human power or wealth to avoid it. The Psalms emphasize this point:

"Do not put your trust in princes, in human beings, who cannot save. When their spirit departs, they return to the ground; on that very day their plans come to nothing" (Psalms 146:3-4, NIV).

This passage underscores the inevitability of death and the inability of human efforts to prevent it. It also serves as a reminder to place trust and hope in God, who alone holds the power over life and death.

The Hope Beyond Death

While the Bible teaches that death is the end of conscious existence, it also offers hope through the promise of resurrection. Jesus Christ, through his sacrifice and resurrection, demonstrated that death does not have to be the final word. For those who put their faith in God and believe what the Bible teaches, there is the assurance of life beyond the grave. Jesus himself said:

"Do not be amazed at this, for a time is coming when all who are in their graves will hear his voice and come out—those who have done what is good will rise to live, and those who have done what is evil will rise to be condemned" (John 5:28-29, NIV).

This hope of resurrection brings comfort to those grieving the loss of a loved one. Death, while painful and final in the human sense, is not permanent in God's plan. (For more scriptural teachings about resurrection, see Chapter 17: The Resurrection Hope.)

A Source of Comfort

Understanding the biblical perspective on death can provide a foundation for enduring the grief that accompanies the loss of a loved one. Recognizing that death is a temporary state and that God has a purpose for all humankind allows for a sense of peace and hope. This perspective shifts the focus from fear or despair to trust in God's promises.

Conclusion

The Bible teaches that death is a return to dust and a state of unconsciousness, without pain or awareness. However, it also assures believers of the hope of resurrection and the promise of eternal life through Jesus Christ. By turning to the Bible for guidance, we find answers to one of life's greatest questions and the reassurance that, in God's hands, death is not the end.

This understanding allows those mourning a spouse to grieve with hope, confident in the knowledge that the same God who created life will one day restore it. As the prophet Isaiah beautifully expressed:

"he will swallow up death forever. The Sovereign Lord will wipe away the tears from all faces; he will

remove his people's disgrace from all the earth The Lord has spoken." (Isaiah 25:8, NIV)

This victory over death is a cornerstone of the Christian faith and a source of solace for those navigating the deep waters of grief. In the next chapter, we will reflect on the journey of grief and growth, offering a roadmap for continuing to honor your past while embracing the endless potential of tomorrow.

Chapter 16: Reflection and Growth

As you near the conclusion of this journey through grief, it is important to reflect on the path you have walked and acknowledge the growth you have achieved. Grieving the loss of a spouse is one of the most profound challenges anyone can face, yet within the struggle lies the potential for transformation. In this chapter, we will look back at what has been learned, celebrate the progress you have made, and explore how to carry these lessons into the future with courage and purpose.

The Power of Reflection

Reflection is a way of honoring both your grief and your healing. It allows you to acknowledge the depth of your loss while also recognizing your resilience and capacity to grow:

- **Acknowledge the Pain:** Reflecting on your journey doesn't mean avoiding the sorrow you have experienced. Instead, it means giving yourself permission to honor your emotions and validate your grief.

- **Recognize Your Strength:** Consider the challenges you have faced and how you have met them. Even small steps forward represent acts of courage and resilience.

- **Appreciate the Journey:** Grief is not linear, and your path may have included setbacks and breakthroughs. Each moment has contributed to your growth.

Lessons Learned Along the Way

Through the experience of loss, you may have uncovered profound insights about yourself, your relationships, and the world around you:

1. **The Depth of Love:**

   - Your grief is a reflection of the love you shared with your spouse. This love remains a part of you, shaping who you are and how you move forward.

2. **The Importance of Support:**

   - Leaning on others—friends, family, or support groups—has shown you the value of connection and vulnerability in times of need.

3. **The Capacity for Resilience:**

   - You have discovered an inner strength you might not have known you possessed. This resilience will serve you well as you continue to face life's challenges.

4. **The Beauty of the Present Moment:**

   - Loss often brings a renewed appreciation for life's small joys and the significance of living fully in the present.

Carrying Growth into the Future

The growth you have experienced through grief can serve as a foundation for a meaningful and fulfilling future. Here are some ways to carry these lessons forward:

1. **Set Intentions for the Future:**

    - Think about what you want to create or experience in the next chapter of your life. Your goals might include fostering relationships, pursuing passions, or simply finding more moments of peace.

2. **Honor Your Spouse's Legacy:**

    - Keep your spouse's memory alive through acts that reflect their values or passions. This could include volunteer work, supporting a cause they cared about, or creating rituals that celebrate their life.

3. **Continue to Seek Growth:**

    - Grief can be a catalyst for self-discovery. Explore new interests, deepen your self-awareness, and remain open to personal transformation.

4. **Embrace Joy Without Guilt:**

   - Finding happiness again does not diminish your love for your spouse. Allow yourself to embrace joy as a sign of your resilience and healing.

A Journey That Continues

The journey of grief does not have a definitive endpoint. Healing is a lifelong process, and your relationship with your loss will evolve over time. Some days may still feel heavy, but others will bring lightness and hope. Each step forward, no matter how small, is a testament to your strength.

- **Trust in Your Resilience:** You have weathered the storm of loss and emerged with a deeper understanding of your own strength and capacity for renewal.

- **Welcome New Chapters:** While you will always carry your spouse's memory with you, there is space for new experiences, relationships, and opportunities in your life.

- **Celebrate Your Journey:** Reflect on how far you have come and take pride in your ability to find meaning and purpose after such a profound loss.

Closing Reflections

Grief is a powerful teacher. It reshapes our lives, tests our limits, and reveals truths about love, resilience, and the human spirit. Through this journey, you have honored your loss while discovering your ability to heal, grow, and thrive.

As you move forward, remember that your grief is a testament to the love you shared and the life you built together. By embracing both the sorrow and the joy, you create a future that honors your past while welcoming the endless potential of tomorrow.

Take each day as it comes, carry the lessons of this journey with you, and trust that hope and healing are always within reach. In the next chapter, we will review the wonderful hope we have of being reunited with our dead loved ones.

Chapter 17: The Resurrection Hope

In the depths of grief, when the pain of losing a spouse feels overwhelming, many turn to their faith for solace and strength. One of the most profound sources of comfort offered in the Bible is the resurrection hope—the promise of a future where death no longer holds sway and where those who have passed will be reunited with their loved ones. This chapter explores the biblical foundation of the resurrection hope, its transformative power in the grieving process, and how it provides enduring encouragement for moving forward.

The Biblical Foundation of the Resurrection Hope

The promise of resurrection is woven throughout the Scriptures, offering assurance that death is not the final chapter. Key passages illuminate this hope:

- **Jesus' Declaration of the Resurrection:** In John 11:25-26, Jesus says, *"I am the resurrection and the life. The one who believes in me will live, even though they die; and whoever lives by believing in me will never die."* These words, spoken before He raised his friend Lazarus from the dead, affirm His authority over death and His power to bring life.

- **The Resurrection of Christ:** The resurrection of Jesus is the cornerstone of the Christian faith. As Paul writes in 1 Corinthians 15:20-22, *"But Christ has indeed been raised from the dead, the firstfruits of those who have fallen asleep. For since death came through a man, the resurrection of the dead comes also through a man. For as in Adam all die, so in Christ all will be made alive."* Christ's victory over death guarantees the resurrection of His followers.

- **The Promise of Eternal Life:** Revelation 21:4 paints a picture of a restored creation where *"He will wipe every tear from their eyes. There will be no more death or mourning or crying or pain, for the old order of things has passed away."* This vision offers hope for a future free from suffering and separation due to death.

How the Resurrection Hope Comforts Grieving Hearts

The resurrection hope brings comfort to those grieving a profound loss in several key ways:

1. **Reassurance of Reunion:**

   - The promise of resurrection assures believers that they will see their loved ones again in paradise on earth. (Psalms 37:29; Isaiah 65:21-25) This reassurance eases the pain of separation, knowing it is temporary. The Bible assures us that there is going to be a resurrection of both the righteous and the wicked. (Acts 24:15)

2. **A New Perspective on Death:**

- For Christians, death is not an end but a transition. Jesus describes it in John 11:11 as sleep, He said, *"Our friend Lazarus has fallen asleep; but I am going there to wake him up."* Here Jesus was speaking about the death and resurrection of his friend Lazarus. This understanding reframes death as a step closer to eternal life.

3. **Strength to Endure Grief:**

- The resurrection hope does not eliminate the sorrow of loss but provides strength to endure it. It reminds believers that God's promises are faithful and true, offering a foundation of hope during the darkest times.

4. **Encouragement to Live Fully:**

- Knowing that eternal life awaits encourages individuals to live with purpose and gratitude, cherishing each moment while holding onto the promise of what is to come.

Living in the Light of the Resurrection Hope

The resurrection hope is not only about the future; it also transforms how believers live in the present. Here are practical ways to embrace this hope:

1. **Cultivate a Deep Connection with God:**

   - Engage in prayer, Bible reading, and worship to strengthen your faith and find solace in God's promises for the future.

2. **Lean on Your Faith Community:**

   - Surround yourself with fellow believers who can offer encouragement, pray with you, and remind you of the hope you share. (Hebrews 10:24-25)

3. **Reflect on God's Faithfulness:**

   - Look back on how God has been present in your life and how His promises have been fulfilled. This reflection can deepen your trust in His purpose for the future. (Isaiah 41:10, 13)

4. **Find Purpose in the Waiting:**

- While longing for the future resurrection, seek ways to honor your loved one's memory and serve others, reflecting God's love and grace in your actions. Perhaps you can volunteer in your local community to help others in need. Acts 20:35 reports Jesus' words that: *"...There is more happiness in giving than there is in receiving".*

Stories of Resurrection Hope

Hearing how others have found comfort in the resurrection hope can inspire and uplift. Consider these examples:

- A woman grieving her husband's death found peace by meditating on 1 Thessalonians 4:13-14, which reminds believers not to grieve *"like the rest of mankind, who have no hope."* This passage gave her the strength to face each day, confident in their eventual reunion.

- A man mourning the loss of his wife started a small group in his church to study the promise of the resurrection. Through this, he found healing and deepened his understanding of God's eternal purpose.

A Closing Word of Hope

The resurrection hope does not erase the pain of losing a spouse, but it provides a lens through which to view that pain—a lens that reveals God's promise of eternal life and reunion. As you navigate the complexities of grief, let this hope anchor your soul, giving you strength to endure, peace to sustain you, and a reason to look forward with anticipation.

In the light of the resurrection hope, grief becomes a testament to love, and loss is transformed into a longing for a future filled with joy, restoration, and the presence of God in your life.

Conclusion: A Journey, Not a Destination

Grief is not a linear process. It does not follow a set timeline or arrive with a clear ending. Instead, it is a journey—a deeply personal path shaped by the love shared and the loss experienced. For those mourning the loss of a spouse, this journey may feel especially heavy, as the person who shared your dreams, your struggles, and your everyday moments is no longer physically present. But while the pain of grief is undeniable, so too is the potential for growth, healing, and hope.

This book has explored the multifaceted nature of grief—the initial shock, the emotional turbulence, the enduring love that shapes the depth of loss, and the role of faith, community, and resilience in navigating the pain. As you reflect on your own journey, remember that grief is not a burden to "get over" but a testament to the love and connection you shared. That love, though it may look different now, remains a part of you.

Honoring the Past, Embracing the Future

Honoring the memory of your loved one is an essential part of the healing process. Their life, their influence, and the moments you shared together are treasures that no loss can take away. By allowing yourself to cherish those memories, you create a bridge between the past and the future.

Moving forward does not mean forgetting or replacing the love you lost. Instead, it means finding ways to carry that love with you as you step into new chapters of your life. This might involve creating traditions to honor their memory, sharing their stories with others, or pursuing goals that reflect the dreams you once shared.

The Role of Faith and Hope

For many, faith provides the foundation to endure grief. The Biblical promises of comfort, restoration, and the resurrection hope offer an anchor for the soul during times of profound sorrow. Knowing that your loved one is in God's care and that a future reunion awaits can transform the weight of loss into a sense of anticipation. It reminds us that death is not the end but a transition into a greater future of everlasting life.

As you lean into these truths, you may find that faith does more than sustain you — it empowers you. It enables you to see beyond the present pain and to trust in God's plan, even when it is hard to understand. Through prayer, Scripture, and fellowship, you can find strength for today and hope for tomorrow.

A New Perspective on Life

Grief has a way of changing us. It shifts our perspective, clarifies our priorities, and reminds us of life's fragility and beauty. Wise King Solomon expressed this thought beautifully in the Bible:

It is better to go to a house of mourning than to go to a house of feasting, for death is the destiny of every-

one; the living should take this to heart. (Ecclesiastes 7:2)NIV

As you navigate this journey, you may discover a deeper appreciation for the present moment and a renewed sense of purpose. Whether it's through nurturing relationships, pursuing passions, or simply savoring life's small joys, grief can lead to a fuller, more intentional way of living.

This transformation is not about diminishing the loss but about integrating it into your life. It's about allowing the pain to shape you in ways that bring wisdom, compassion, and strength. In this way, grief becomes not just a reflection of what was lost but also a testament to what remains—love, faith, and the capacity for hope.

The Journey Continues

As you move forward, know that grief will revisit you at times. Milestones, anniversaries, or unexpected moments may bring waves of sorrow. These moments are not setbacks but reminders of the depth of your connection. Allow yourself to feel, to remember, and to honor your emotions as they arise.

Remember, too, that you are not alone. Whether through faith, family, friends, or a supportive community, there are people who care about you and want to walk alongside you. Seek their support, and when you are ready, offer your support to others who are grieving. In doing so, you will find that sharing your journey can bring healing and connection.

A Final Word of Hope

The journey of grief is deeply personal, but it is not without hope. The love you shared with your spouse continues to shape you, and the faith you hold can sustain you. Most importantly, the resurrection hope promises that the story is not over. As Revelation 21:4 assures us, there will come a day when *"He will wipe every tear from their eyes. There will be no more death or mourning or crying or pain, for the old order of things has passed away."*

Until that day, take each step forward with courage and grace. Let the love you carry and the faith you hold guide you. Grief is not a destination to reach but a journey to travel—one that can lead to healing, transformation, and the enduring promise of hope.

About the Author

Janice A. Campbell is a native New Yorker but now lives on Vancouver Island, British Columbia in Canada. She graduated from Hunter College HS in 1971, and from Massachusetts Institute of Technology in 1975 with a BS in mathematics. She worked as a financial systems analyst in three Fortune 500 companies. Since 1986 she has been a Christian minister. She has traveled extensively in the United States, preaching and teaching others about the Bible and God's Kingdom.

She is the stepmother of three adults, grandmother of five, and great-grandmother of two toddlers. She has endured the deaths of her parents, older sister, and her husband. This book fulfills her desire to create a memorial to the love she shared with her husband and, as a Christian minister, to ease the suffering of others enduring the loss of their spouse.

Made in the USA
Las Vegas, NV
20 February 2025